- THE DOCTOR IS IN -

DOCTOR

NERDLOVE

DATING ADVICE

FOR THE MODERN NERD

- SINCE 2011 -

Other Books By Harris O'Malley

New Game + : A Geek's Guide to Love, Sex and Dating
When It Clicks: The Guide To Mastering Online Dating
Simplified Dating: The Ultimate Guide To Getting Better at Dating…
Quickly!

IT'S DANGEROUS TO GO ALONE
A RELATIONSHIP SURVIVAL HANDBOOK

Harris O'Malley

NERDLOVE PUBLICATIONS

To Cat.

Always.

What I Wish I'd Known Before My First Relationship

One of the great paradoxes of dating is that we tend to focus a lot on the early stages of love. We put our focus on becoming someone desirable, on finding the "right" person and enjoying the magical process of falling in love.

Of course, once we succeed and find ourselves *in* a relationship, then we tend to find ourselves lost at sea. Like Inigo Monotya, we've spent so much time seeking this goal that now that we've achieved it, we have no idea what to do with ourselves.

To be honest, it's not that surprising. We live in a culture that's in love with the concept of falling in love. Pop culture is obsessed with the idea of the meet cute and the story of the happy couple getting together. It's considerably less interested in what it takes for a couple to *stay* together. No matter where you turn, you'll find stories about happy couples meeting, falling for one another, overcoming the obstacles in their way and then...

And that's it. There's the kiss. The wedding. The little coded signifiers of "yup, they're a couple now," and then we leave them to what we assume is surely a "happily ever after". *The Legend of Korra*'s Korra and Asami hold hands and head out on their next adventure. Han Solo and Leia's arc ends in *Return of the Jedi* with a final reminder that they love each other and now they're likely going to get married.[1] Veronica Mars and Logan Echols get another reminder that they're fated for one another. Kaylee Fry and Simon Tam end their story in post-coital bliss after a season's worth of sexual tension and near-misses.

And we, the audience, are left to assume that nothing bad happens to them afterwards. We almost never see what happens to the couple after the end of the book or the credits roll. On the rare occasions we do check back, we only see the aftermath of "something happened" and now they're single again. Han and Leia are no longer together because "something happened"[2]. Mulder and Scully got divorced because of events that will only be hinted at. Peter Venkman and Dana Barrett couldn't make it work. Indiana Jones and Marion Ravenwood[3] split up because of reasons we'll never see.

As a result: we have damned few models for how relationships work. If we're lucky enough to have parents in a happy marriage, then we might have a clue. But more and more often, once we've found a partner, we discover we've been tossed into the deep end of the pool and expected to learn to swim as best we can. At my site, *Paging Dr. NerdLove*, one of the most common refrains I hear from people is "I have no idea what I'm doing right now, but I'm pretty sure I'm doing it wrong."

This is especially true when you're dealing with your first serious relationship. You're fumbling around in the dark, trying to make the adjustments that come when you start to share your life with another person. My first serious relationship was full of avoidable mistakes and disasters that one might charitably call "learning experiences"[4] because I had no fucking clue what I was doing. I was terrified and had nowhere to turn because, honestly, most of my peers didn't have any more of an idea than I did.

Here's a secret though: all relationships are functionally like a first relationship. Every relationship is a matter of getting to know the other person, making your lifestyles and expectations mesh, learning how to tolerate each other's little quirks etc. The only difference is that people who've had other relationships (hopefully) have the experience to guide them through the rough patches. Even then, however, we'll often find ourselves in situations where we're utterly and completely lost. What does this argument really mean? Does this feeling mean that our relationship is fatally flawed? Is this a bump in the road, or is this the beginning of the end?

But that's why I'm here: to help you navigate through the complex, twisted and often scary world of relationships so that hopefully you can avoid the most common mistakes. That way you can make new and different mistakes.

But joking aside: relationships are work and no matter what the songs have told you, love really isn't all you need. But with this guide, you'll have a template to follow to help ease you through the trials and tribulations that come with being part of a couple.

I won't lie to you: relationships can be tough. They can be frustrating, even maddening. You'll fight and fuck, you'll love each other with the passion of a thousand suns and you'll want to be with anyone *but* them. But at the end of the day, you'll know how to come together to fight past the low points and sail through the high points. You'll walk through the fire, hand in hand, and come out stronger than tempered steel on the other side.

And then, the two of you will be able to build your own happily ever after... together.

---

[1] And then *The Force Awakens* happened.

[2] Admittedly, your son going to the Dark Side and murdering a whole bunch of people is going to strain any relationship...

[3] Incidentally, what *is* it about Harrison Ford that we keep wanting to see him having broken up with his love interests?

[4] A less charitable person would call it "a profound series of

catastrophes"

PART ONE:
THE HONEYMOON PERIOD

The early days of a relationship are among the most magical for a couple. At this stage, love is quite literally a drug. Your brain is mainlining dopamine and norepinephrine and everything your partner does is goddamn *magical*. You want to spend as much time in their presence as possible because you *really* want another hit.

In practical, non-romantic terms, your brain is trying to get you to spend as much time with your new squeeze. This way, as you start getting habituated to the dopamine, the oxytocin has a chance to kick in. Now you may not be getting the same butterflies-and-adrenaline kick to the system when you see your sweetie, but those chemicals are encouraging the two of you to bond.

In these heady, early days, it's hard to be rational about things because, goddamn it, everything feels so good. Everything about your partner is amazing and perfect and you can't imagine they'd ever break your heart or that there's a part of them that isn't made up of pizza and rainbows. But getting metaphorically high in their presence is a lot like being literally high: your brain isn't working at peak efficiency. You get caught up in the rush and make a lot of decisions you might not otherwise make in the cold light of (metaphorical) sobriety.

Everyone's judgement at this stage gets hazy because our amygdala kinda shuts down and we end up eliding over a whole bunch of things that might be red flags (or at least caution signals). It feels totally rational and sensible, but — like a frat boy deciding after four Tuaca Bombs that now is the perfect time to sing "Shimmy Shimmy Ya" at karaoke — what seems like a good idea at the time doesn't necessarily pan out later.

So while you're enjoying the honeymoon stage of your relationship, it's important to start building the habits and patterns *now* that will help solidify your relationship down the line as things settled down and you become more serious.

In this section, I'm going to teach you about the things that will make sure this relationship has what it takes to go the distance. From the universal truths of *every* relationship to the conversations you should be having before you make it Facebook Official, this is all about building a solid foundation to that you can use to build the *rest* of your relationship upon.

ONE

FIVE UNIVERSAL RELATIONSHIP TRUTHS

From Your First Relationship To Your Last

EVERY RELATIONSHIP IS going to be special and different in it's own way. Even if you have your "type", each person you date is going to be unique and every relationship is going to be a process of discovery and revelation. Your partner will surprise you, confuse you, confound you and delight you in ways you'll never be able to expect or anticipate over the course of your time together.

That having been said, however, there are certain universalities that are going to be true across every relationship. From your first relationship to your last — whenever that may be — every relationship is going to be bound by certain truths. It's part of the human experience and something that's going to be true across cultures, genders, sexual preferences and experience levels.

The problem is that, more often than not, we tend to mistake these truths for flaws within the relationship. Until we've had enough experience to recognize these experiences for what they truly are, we tend to assume that they're indicators that something's gone wrong. We've chosen the wrong partner, we've started falling out of love with them, our love isn't strong enough to overcome the issues, there's something wrong with us… it's a recipe for generating vast amounts of pointless anxiety. Worse, it can often lead to ending a relationship when we didn't actually need to.

Ideally, with time and experience, we come to recognize these facts as simply part of the price of being in a relationship with another person who has the nerve to be as imperfect as we are. But part of my job as a dating coach is to help people avoid needless pain and anxiety, so they can focus on enjoying being with their partners. So let's talk a little about what you can expect in every relationship you'll ever have.

That New Relationship Energy Is Going To Fade

One of the most important lessons to learn early on is that every relationship has it's honeymoon period where everything is perfect and amazing. This is often referred to as the "new relationship energy" and it's the emotional equivalent of that new car smell. Every single thing about them is special and perfect and a reminder that you couldn't be luckier than you currently are. Your heart starts skipping a beat every time you think of them and you can't keep your hands off each other because there's literally nothing more erotic than just being in the room with them.

This is also why the first six months or so of your first relationship are the worst time to make any long-term (or even medium term) decisions about the state of your relationship. You're in a love haze that short-circuits your higher logic functions. Intellectually you may know that your judgement isn't clear, but your heart (and groin) are busy telling your brain that it doesn't know what the hell it's talking about and it needs to get on the love train already. This is part of why everyone at the start of a new relationship is a blithering idiot whose sole purpose in life is to annoy all their friends with how shmoopy the two of them can be.

The trouble is that quite literally everything in your brain and body was conspiring to make you a twitterpated moron. Just as that new car smell is actually the off-gassing of the chemicals used in manufacturing the car in the first place, that new relationship energy is an intoxicating rush of hormones and endorphins that turn off your higher functions. You're too busy being flooded with phenylethylamine, dopamine and norepinephrine firing off every neuron in the pleasure centers of your brain and convincing you that the way your girlfriend chews her food is is goddamn amazing to think clearly. Everything is floating hearts, cartoon birds and winged babies floating all around you and making you feel that the universe itself is smiling directly on you and any second the world around you is going to burst out into a song and dance number.

The thing to keep in mind is this happens almost *every single time.* We may associate that first relationship rush with being young – our high-school or college years. But even grown-ass adults can and do get caught up in the emotional roller-coaster ride that is starting a relationship with someone new.

But as much fun as it is to get lost in the rush of that initial infatuation, you have to be careful. See, much like the guy at the casino who's had five Jack and Cokes and thinks he's got a perfect system for beating roulette, when you're in the throes of that new relationship energy, your common sense tends to go right out the window. It's not uncommon to let that dopamine high lead you to make plans that may well not stand the test of time. In the first months of the relationship, you simply don't know each other well enough – no matter how convinced you are that nobody has ever felt like this before about somebody else. That decision to move in together may seem perfect in the dopamine haze, but falls apart when it fades and his or her inability to clean up after themselves isn't cute anymore.

Of course, the other issue is that this rush fades in time. Doesn't matter who you are or how intense your feelings are for your new partner; the half-life of that initial infatuation is six months to a year. After that, the passion and intensity starts to diminish.

This doesn't mean that your feelings have changed or that something's wrong; it just means that you've adapted. The Borg Collective of your brain has assimilated your new experience and now it's simply part of your every day life. Believe it or not, this is simply how our brains work. One of the quirks of the human experience is that we can get used to *anything*. The hormones taper off, the novelty dwindles and an effect known as "hedonic adaptation" kicks in. What was new and exciting has become commonplace. It's now part of your every day life and it's simply not going to excite you the way it used to. However, because that passion has changed, couples panic. They worry that they're falling out of love or that they never had that connected in the first place.

It's important to not mistake the rush for the *relationship*. That rush that brought you together is exciting, but shallow. Over your time, your connection deepens into a stronger commitment based on emotional intimacy and affection, not *just* passion. It's part of the life cycle of every romantic relationship, not a sign that things have gone wrong. Once you recognize that change for what it really is, you won't fear the change; instead you'll recognize it as your relationship moving to a new and equally exciting level.

You're Both Going To Want to Bang Other People

There are two issues that I see over and over again that sink otherwise happy relationships. The first is money. The second is monogamy. Of the two, I'd go so far as to say that monogamy is the bigger problem. There are, after all, far fewer restrictions about talking about money issues in a relationship.

The problem with monogamy is, frankly, the conflict between what society tells us and what reality tells us. In western culture, monogamy is seen as the default state of romance; if you truly love someone, then there's no room for anyone else. If you start to stray or find yourself falling for someone else, then obviously you were never truly in love with your first partner, else you would never leave.

This, unfortunately, is bullshit. It makes for a lovely story to tell people about sex and relationships, but the reality on the ground is considerably different, and this causes no end of unnecessary strife for couples. I see come up again and again in my line of work. Couples — especially from people who've had relatively little dating experience — realize that they're having naughty thoughts about other people and begin to panic. Suddenly, everything's in a massive crisis; they don't know why they're having these sweaty thoughts about Carol in Accounting or Jake, the barista who makes the best lattes, but they're terrified about what it means.

What it means is that you're a primate with a functioning sex drive. That's *it*.

One of the biggest lies we tell ourselves as a culture is that monogamy is natural and easy. That if you desire other people besides the person you love, then you're doing something wrong. In reality, this goes against literally everything our bodies were designed to do.

If you strip away the romance and the complicated societal rules and general philosophical meandering, humanity's purpose is very simple: we're here to ensure the continuation of our genetic lineage. Full stop. As a result: we crave sexual variety in order to ensure that we — men and women both — spread our genes far and wide. Our very bodies evolved with the idea of multiple sexual partners in mind. The chemical rush that we get from sex with the same partner over and over again diminishes over time[1], only to return to original levels when we sleep with someone new. Scientists theorize that part of the point of a woman's orgasm is to cause vocalizations, which attract other men to come and mate as well — not only increasing the odds of successful impregnation, but also obscuring the parentage to encourage a communal responsibility for the child. Meanwhile, the flared glans of the penis acts like a squeegee inside the vaginal canal, scraping out seminal fluid from a woman's previous partner. Similarly, male primates who believe that there is a chance that their partner has recently had sex with another male will actually produce a greater volume of ejaculate in order to flush out a competitor's sperm. Hell, there have been studies that suggest that humans have goddamn hunter/killer sperm cells -- ones that can't actually penetrate the ovum but instead serve to block other people's sperm like tiny linebackers.

And this is without getting into how humans are among only three mammalian species[2] that have sex strictly for pleasure, the importance of sex in fostering communal bonds via the generation of oxytocin and a host of other issues that are far outside the scope of this book[3].

Traditional monogamy[4] is not our natural state; it goes against everything our bodies and instincts have evolved to do. That isn't to say that monogamy is bad, wrong or undesirable, simply that it's *difficult*. Being monogamous is a choice, not a magical spell that eliminates desire for anyone other than your partner. No matter how much you love your partner, you're *going* to be attracted to other people. You're going to get hit with crushes out of the clear blue sky that'll make you feel like a giggly teenager again. You'll meet people who get you *so* revved up that you'll have trouble walking in their presence. That is entirely, *perfectly* normal. It happens to everyone. Your partner is going to have those same sudden infatuations and attractions as you are. It doesn't mean that you're not enough for them or that they're unsatisfied with you. It's just part of the human experience.

Just remember: attraction *isn't* an obligation nor is arousal a compulsion. The fact that you find yourself attracted to someone doesn't mean that you need to act on it with that person. In fact, part of the fun of being in a relationship is enjoying the giggly energy that comes from a crush or from an unexpected attraction and plowing it into your relationship with your partner.

You're Going To Fight. Don't Freak Out About It

The first road bump on the road to love for relationship newbies tends to be the First Fight. Up until this point, everything has been smooth sailing where the harshest disagreement you've had is "who is more schmoopy". And then one of you says something wrong over take out Pad-Thai and suddenly there's yelling and there's crying and everything is falling apart!?! WHAT DO YOU DO?

Well, you chill out, Beavis. *Fights* happen. They're a part of relationships. Put two people together with their own wants and desires and you're inevitably going to have conflict. There's really no way to insulate yourself from this. No relationship goes on *without* butting heads over some random issue or another. It doesn't matter how perfect your partner may be, how hot they are, how sweet or how giving. As a sage one said, behind every incredible human being is someone who is utterly *fed up* with their shit.

The fact that you're having a fight really doesn't say anything about the strength or validity of your relationship. In fact, too many people tend to treat *not* fighting as a virtue — as though avoiding conflict means that you're both perfectly in sync. In reality, all never fighting usually means is that someone's letting themselves get walked all over and is afraid to express themselves. This ain't any healthier than a couple who are *always* fighting.

At the same time, how *often* you're fighting doesn't necessarily mean that your relationship is in trouble either. Some couples *enjoy* having vigorous debates and discussions. Other times, both partners may be very passionate people and their "fight/make-up" routine is simply a part of their relationship dynamic. As long as both parties aren't fighting to *wound* - attacking each other in the vulnerable areas that only a long-term partner would know, saying things just to be hurtful, etc. — and have functionally opted-in to the dynamic... well, it's not a relationship style *I* would have chosen, but if they're both happy, more power to 'em.

The *right* question to ask is what you're fighting about and *how* you're fighting. If you're going to fight — and, again, it *will* happen — then you want to aim to resolve the source of conflict, not simply to score points to get the title of Least Wrong.

The most important thing to keep in mind is very simple: don't let the anger linger. A lot of people will tell you "never go to bed angry", which sounds wise, but it isn't actually helpful in and of itself. Taking this too literally tends to encourage trying to end the fight and suppress how you're feeling, rather than actually resolving the underlying issue.

Instead *it's* better to never go to bed without reminding each other that you love one another. Yeah, they may be dancing on your last nerve and all you want is to explode like Vesuvius all over them, but *you still love them.* Just, y'know. Deep down. Really deep. Possibly requiring excavating equipment.

Getting to that core of love and affection you have for your partner is important. Don't let your anger blind you to the fact that you're with them because of how wonderful and special they are to you.

No matter how much you may want to rip their goddamn head off right now.

Don't worry if all of this seems complicated. I'll be teaching you all about how to fight the *right* way in chapter 8.

Your Partner's Had Relationships Before You... And There's a Reason Why They're With You Now

It is incredibly rare that you are going to find yourself in a relationship with someone who has never dated anyone else before. It *does* happen, but the odds are so astronomical that you're more likely to win the Powerball AND get your favorite Mondo poster at the same time.

However, the idea that your partner has had other relationships and (gasp, shock) had *sex* with other people seems to throw some people into a panic spiral. In my experience as a dating coach, I find this happens most often among men — occasionally women too, but primarily men — who are in their first relationship. They tend to be worried about the differences in experience levels; they feel that their inexperience is somehow a disqualifier. They worry that they couldn't possibly measure up to her previous lovers because they don't know as much or have done as much. It's a classic Catch-22; they feel that they can't get into a relationship because they don't have the experience, but they can't get the experience without the relationship.

Other times they worry that the more experienced partner is not going to respect them because they'll have never dated anyone before and this means that something's wrong with them. Still other times, they become concerned that they will never be able to measure up to a partner's previous lovers — this one was handsomer, this one was richer, this one was a better kisser, this one had bigger boobs or a larger cock or some other nebulous quality that the person agonizing doesn't have. The details vary, but it almost always leads to the same place: being convinced your partner can never be satisfied with you because *fuck you, that's why.*

In almost every case, this anxiety relies on mistaken ideas about the nature of attraction and why folks date the people they do. Relationships aren't comparison shopping. Women don't choose to date someone because they used to have a Boyfriend 3 and now they'll only take a Boyfriend 6s Plus. Men aren't continually looking for an upgrade over their previous girlfriend. People aren't attracted to someone because they hit a certain number of checkmarks on a list; they're attracted to that person because of the qualities that make them uniquely them.

Ok, I take that back. Some people *do* make a point of trying to date like they're upgrading their cellphones and only want the newest, hottest model. We call those people assholes. Quit worrying about the dating habits of assholes. They will inevitably do you the favor of *not* dating you, which will be the greatest gift they can give you.

Do some people consider a lack of relationship experience a flaw? Yes… but we judge people on the holistic person, not on their specs list as though we're trying to decide between an Xbox and a Playstation. Yes, a person will have their faults, but do their other qualities make up for it? And if that theoretical person considers your lack of dating experience to be a flaw then they have done you a favor because you don't want to date them. As with assholes, they will have self-selected out of your dating pool and you should be grateful.

Seriously. Someone should make greeting cards for that.

Similarly, when you're dating someone who has had relationships before (and most people have), you're not competing with their exes. You're not competing with *anyone*. They aren't dating you because you're a better lover, dresser or prepare a *croque monsieur* better than everyone they've ever dated. They're dating you because you're *you*, with all of the little quirks that make you who you are.

How do you get past these fears with your partner? Simple: you communicate, communicate, communicate. Use your words. Let them know that you have this anxiety – not because it's their problem but because you want them to understand where your head's at. Work together to find a way that they can reassure you and calm those anxieties.

And when they do, take yes for a goddamn answer.

Every Relationship Ends Until One Doesn't

OK, it's time for some straight talk: all relationships end, eventually. Except when they don't. And you can never be sure which one that will be.

To be sure, nobody likes to think about their relationship being temporary after all, and going into a relationship assuming that you're going to break up eventually is the opposite of romance. But at the same time, pretending that this isn't a possibility doesn't do you any good either.

People have a tendency to misunderstand relationships and break-ups. We usually enter into each relationship with the assumption that this is the last one we will ever have... and that's a mistake. That mindset stresses us out and makes every conflict seem like one of catastrophic importance because "what if this means that we won't last until the end of time!!!!" because we assume the the fail-state of relationships is "break up".

Except breaking up with someone doesn't mean that the relationship was a failure. The fact that you didn't stay together until one of you died in the saddle doesn't mean that the relationship didn't work, that the two of you weren't right for each other or that either of you did anything wrong. Not every relationship is *meant* to be a lifelong one. Not every love story is going to be an epic poem. Some are short stories. Some are dirty limericks. And that's *fine*.

Don't get me wrong: I'm not saying that you should enter every relationship with the idea that it's doomed to failure. Quite the opposite; you should enter your relationship with the idea that you're going to savor and appreciate every moment.

I know, I know. Stick with me, this will all make sense in a moment.

We all grow and change as people and we don't necessarily have complete control over how we grow. Sometimes we grow apart from people or outgrow our relationships. That doesn't mean that the relationship itself was a failure. All that's happened is that this particular relationship has run its natural course and now it's time to move to the next stage of our lives. Take a look back at some of your earliest relationships with the perspective and experience you have now. Odds are that you'll recognize that while that relationship was right for that part of your life, it could never work with who you are at this point and time.

That's one of the reasons why it's important to appreciate every moment with your partner — just because a relationship ended doesn't mean that it wasn't important or enjoyable or that you didn't learn from it or that your partner wasn't someone special to you.

A successful relationship doesn't mean staying with someone until you die, nor does avoiding a break-up make a relationship successful. You can stay in a relationship that makes you soul-crushingly miserable until the day they carry you out in a pine box. Personally, I'd call *that* a failed relationship over the couple that realized they were done and made a clean break of it.

In fact, if you can part on good terms with your ex and stay friends, then I would call that a successful relationship, even though you broke up. If you can appreciate the good times in your relationship, if you see it as having been good for you in the long run and savor those memories, then how is that anything *but* a success? You've both grown as people but you have also held on to the affection, intimacy and friendship that brought you together in the first place. That, in and of itself is something astounding and to be celebrated.

So yes, your relationship — whether it's your first or simply your latest — may well *not* be your last. But that doesn't mean that an ending is something to be feared. Appreciate your relationship for what it is. Enjoy and savor every moment, even when things aren't at their peak. If and when it does end, then yes, go ahead and mourn it. It's sad when relationships end[5]. But the fact that it ended doesn't magically negate all the good times that you shared together, or that this person was someone special in your life.

And as the pain subsides, you will realize that everything you learned in your first relationship is what helps make you ready for your next relationship.

OK, so enough downer talk. Instead, let's talk about making things *work*.

---

[1] This is known as the Coolidge Effect; we'll be going into this in more detail in later chapters.

[2] Along with bonobos and dolphins...

[3] It's actually kind of fascinating. If you're at all interested in the subject, I'd recommend reading *Sex at Dawn* by Christopher Ryan and Cathilda Jethá

[4] Which, interestingly, has changed over the years. Monogamy *used* to mean "one partner *ever*." Now it means "one at a time".

[5] Most of the time, anyway. Other times you'll dance around the room with a celebratory Scotch, singing "Ding Dong The Witch Is Dead".

...not that I've ever done this.

Two
DEFINING THE RELATIONSHIP

The Dreaded DTR

ONE OF THE hardest moments in any relationship is simply establishing that you're in one. Straight talk: there are two phrases in any relationship that can send paroxysms of terror into anyone. The first is "We need to talk." The second is "Where do you think this relationship is going?" Frankly, more people would rather hear that the dead are rising from the grave and, by the way, you may have been bitten, then start the dreaded "Defining The Relationship" talk.

The DTR talk has achieved an almost mythical level of terror amongst people — even people who *want* commitment — because it almost always comes at the worst possible moment. Suddenly, you find yourself in the position of having to make decisions that will define the two of you for the rest of your relationship.

Even if you're actively hoping to be able to make the official Facebook status change to "In A Relationship...", having the "Defining The Relationship" conversation can be rife with anxiety and potential pitfalls. When do you bring it up? Is a month too soon? Is three months too late? What do you do if you say you want to be serious... and they don't? What if you've completely misunderstood the nature of your relationship? Guys always talk about the Overly Attached Girlfriend... but what if *you're* the Overly Attached Boyfriend? And just what does it mean when they want to "keep things casual"? What about if they're looking "for something serious"? POP QUIZ HOT SHOT, WHAT DO YOU DO?

You calm down, that's what. The reason that the DTR conversation is so terrifying is because we almost always do it *wrong*. The key to acing the "Defining The Relationship" talk — whether you're trying to find the right time to bring it up or when it's been sprung on you — is to keep your head instead of letting panic make the decisions for you.

When Is It The Right Time To Have The Talk?

One of the first and most common questions is simply "when should you have the defining the relationship" talk?

Well... it depends. As much as it would be nice to have a handy rule of thumb like "three weeks after you start sleeping together" or a concrete date, every relationship is different and, as a result, the timing will be different as well. However, as with navigating the tricky world of gift giving in a new relationship there are some guidelines as to whether to have it sooner or later.

It may help to think of your relationship as a statistic in a role-playing game — the more the "relationship" meter fills up, the more appropriate it becomes to have the talk and decide just where this relationship is going. Different factors are going to make that meter progress at different rates. For example:

1) How often have you been seeing each other?

Dating is a cumulative experience; the more often you see each other, the more likely that you're going to want to define what you have sooner rather than later. When you're seeing each other once or twice a week at the most — especially if it's just on weekends — there is a lower level of implied intimacy and emotional investment than a couple that sees each other three to four times a week. Two people who're making a point of seeing each other whenever they can carries an implication that they're moving towards something committed. People who have a simple fuck-buddy relationship — where you're both enjoying the sex but you're not interested in more — don't tend to spend a lot of time together. In fact, if you've been finding that you're seeing each other more and more often lately, that's often a sign that you're both becoming more and more interested in one another and invested in your relationship together – a sign that you should consider discussing just where you think the relationship is going.

The amount of time you spend together when you do see each other should be factored in as well. After all, we all have lives that can get in the way of our plans. If you can only get together once every couple of weeks, but you spend hours together when you do, then odds are that you're going to be having the conversation sooner rather than later. On the other hand, if you're getting together twice or three times a week on your lunch break, but not spending extended periods of time together, then the DTR talk can be pushed back in the relationship timeline.

Similarly, a couple that only sees each other in short, intense bursts in between long stretches of non-contact (long-distance relationships and out-of-town hook-ups, for example) is probably going to want to have the DTR conversation sooner, if only to make sure that you're both on the same page. The intensity of that time together, coupled with the length of time spent when you are together can affect how you see the relationship and where you see it going. Some long-distance couples might want to define the relationship after the third visit, because they're spending weeks at a time together whenever they see each other.

2) How Often Do You Communicate Outside of Your Dates?

Time spent in person isn't the only measure of the progress of the relationship. Just because we may not have face to face contact doesn't mean that we're not still keeping in touch with one another. Email, texting, Snapchats, Google Hangouts, Skype calls, FaceTime and other forms of social media have become part of our collective courtship rituals. In our increasingly connected world, we have more ways of spending time with our dates when we can't necessarily be there in person.

However, it's the quality of that communication that matters more than any other factor. There's a significant difference between occasionally touching base or sharing a funny image on Facebook and having long, involved conversations. On one extreme, you may have two people who's primary mode of communication is liking or commenting on images in their Instagram pages. On the other extreme, couples may use Skype as a telepresence hang-out. They'll start a Skype call and then the two of them will just go about their day.

If you're talking every single day on the phone or over social media between the moments when your schedules line up, it moves the timeline for the DTR conversation slightly to "sooner". If you're not talking much outside of your dates except to set up the next one, then it's safer to leave the conversation for later; your behavior is indicating that you're not quite so invested in the relationship as to need to define things.

Yet.

3) Are You Having Sex?

Sharing bodily fluids and smashing squishy bits together tends to change the equation... but as with most things, it can be highly contextual. For example: most people will see dating someone you haven't had sex with as being less serious. However, there are people who prefer to wait to have sex or who are interested in *romance* but not sex. This can lead to miscommunications and misunderstandings as one partner sees the other as being less interested or less committed.

Having sex in and of itself doesn't mean anything one way or the other, but it can confuse the issue if the two of you aren't on the same page. People who're looking for a committed relationship will be more likely to see sex as taking things "to the next level". People who are looking for something more casual tend to see sex as an end-goal in and of itself.

Unsurprisingly, there are many times when those two people are having sex with each other...

If you are having sex, then it's not a bad idea to at least touch base, if only to manage expectations. This especially if you get the sense that you aren't in agreement about the nature of your relationship. It's better to be honest about how you're feeling than to hide it and end up hurt or disappointing one another because you had different ideas about where this was heading.

If one of you isn't interested in sexual activity or prefers to wait to have sex — whether for personal comfort, reasons of faith or any other reason — then it's better to establish your expectations early on. If you see this as something that is going to lead to a commitment, then it's important to be up front early on. Many people are less likely to stick around, without some idea of how you anticipate things progressing.

One hard and fast rule though: if you haven't had the exclusivity talk, you *aren't* exclusive. Never assume that just because *you* aren't seeing anyone else that they aren't too. If exclusivity is important to you, then you need to establish this early on. otherwise you risk getting hurt, even though you both may have had the best of intentions.

And as a side-note: These guidelines are assuming that the frequency you're seeing each other or talking is a mutual decision. If one of you wants more than the other is providing, it's better to talk it out earlier instead of letting the resentment grow.

Schedule The Talk

Part of why so many people treat the "Defining The Relationship" talk like a cancer diagnosis is because more often than not, it gets sprung on them out of the clear blue sky. This is quite possibly the worst, most counterproductive way to negotiate something as important as the potential future of your relationship together. Very few people — men *or* women — are going to be happy when they feel like they need to make binding decisions about the nature of their relationship with absolutely no warning.

Its also counter-productive; spring the question on someone and they're far more likely to say "no," even if they might otherwise *want* a more committed relationship. While there are people who are incredibly decisive by nature, most people will want a chance to think things over before they decide on something, especially something that changes the nature of their relationship with a person. Even very spontaneous people are going to have an issue making a decision that important without a chance to think things through. As a result: they're far more likely to default to whatever answer maintains the current status-quo.

Worse, when they get hit with the "so where do you see this relationship going?" question, they'll feel under intense pressure to answer the "right" way... and you don't know what the "right" answer is. It's like having a pop-quiz, except failure results in being dumped — either right then and there or in the near future. This is a wonderful recipe for resentment in your relationship. Even if they *want* something serious, nobody likes to feel like they've been pressured into agreeing to something they didn't want because they were caught up in the stress of the moment.

This goes both ways, incidentally. People have said or agreed to things in the moment because of how excited they were that they would never say or do in calmer or more sober moments. This is why discussing the relationship after — or immediately before, or even *during* — isn't a great idea[1]. The things you might think are a great idea while your heart is racing, your blood is pumping and your blood has left your brain to all points south aren't necessarily things you might want if you weren't caught up in the heat of the moment.

The DTR conversation is an important milestone in the course of your relationship , so it's critical that you both have time to *actually* think things through... even if you know the answer already. This is why you want to *schedule* the talk with your partner — it gives them a heads up and picks a specific time and place to talk things out.

For the love of all things holy, however, *don't* broach the topic with the words "we need to talk." That is the almost universal sign of "things are horribly, horribly wrong," and instantly put people in the wrong emotional state. Instead, if you want to have the DTR conversation, tell your partner "Hey, I'd like to talk with you about us and our relationship, figure out where we're going and what this all means. How does Saturday work for you?" Pick a day when you're not going to have any commitments, deadlines or responsibilities that are going to cut into your time together; you want to be able to have the talk when you're both relaxed. The conversation may be short or it may be long but either way, you want to be able to talk about it without feeling like you need to come up with an immediate answer or face the consequences.

If your partner springs the conversation on you without warning, then ask for time to think and pick a day to talk about it. If they're worth dating, they *should* be cool with it. After all, if they care about your feelings on the matter, they will actually respect that you want to give this important discussion the attention it deserves. If they're demanding an answer right then and there… well, they're showing you that they are less concerned with how you feel and more about getting the "right" answer from you. This can be a serious relationship warning sign, so proceed with all due caution.

Define Your Terms

One of the biggest causes of relationship strife is when two people are talking but they're fundamentally speaking two entirely different languages. You may recognize the words, but the meaning behind them is so divergent that neither of you actually understand what the other is saying.

This is doubly true when it comes to having the DTR talk. Different people can have radically different expectations about what's implied by things being "serious" or "casual", what exclusivity means and what lies ahead for the two of you. One person's "casual" means "non-exclusive, sex only" while another's means "we only see each other once a week". *Your* "serious" may mean "sexual exclusivity" while somebody else's means "calling each other boyfriend/girlfriend" while another person's means "We are definitely going to get married."

This is why when you're defining the relationship, you first need to define your terms and expectations. Miscommunication at this phase of your relationship can set the stage for incredible amounts of strife and heartache down the line. After all, it doesn't do you any good to put the effort in to try to establish just where you are if you're not both working from the same map.

It may not feel romantic to be painstaking and exact about meaning and intent when you're trying to say "Yes, this relationship is very important to me and I want to share more of my life with you", but it can help prevent fights before they even happen. Be very upfront with what you want or expect. If you say you want something casual, explain just what you mean by "casual". What do you expect from your partner, and what should they expect from you? Does casual also mean sexual non-exclusivity to you, or does it mean that, while you're not seeing other people, you also aren't necessarily seeing this as leading to a long-term, committed relationship? If you mean "serious", do you mean that you see yourselves on the path to a more involved commitment – moving in together, children, marriage – or that you expect to spend more time together while leaving the future undefined?

If you're not sure what your partner means, then don't be afraid to ask questions. It can feel a little awkward at first — admitting you're not sure what they mean can feel a lot like saying "I r dum" — but it's important to make sure you both understand what the other is saying. After all, the last thing you want to do is to get into an unnecessary argument because you want the same things but you're getting tripped up by the way you aren't using the same words. It's easy to say "words mean what they mean", but that is cold comfort when you end up breaking up because you were unable to communicate exactly what you were thinking.

Stand Up For Yourself

Remember what I said about feeling as though you need to give the "right" answer or else?

When you're having the DTR conversation, the pressure to agree can be intense. This is especially true if you're left feeling as though the fate of your relationship is in the balance. Even if you're both going into the conversation with the best of intentions, it can feel as though one wrong answer can mean hurting the other person and torpedoing what was an otherwise happy and successful relationship.

At the same time however, you don't want to agree to things that will make *you* unhappy in the long run. Letting the relationship continue at the cost of your own long-term happiness isn't a victory by any stretch of the imagination. All you've done is kick your break-up down the road to a time when disentangling yourself is even more difficult and heart-breaking.

This is why it's vitally important to be willing to enforce your boundaries and stand up for yourself and what you need when you're setting the terms of your relationship together. No relationship is going to survive one partner feeling as though they were pushed into something they didn't want but felt obligated to agree to.

Relationships, after all, are partnerships, and you're both equal partners. You want something that feels right to *both* of you, not just one person giving in to the other's wants and desires at the cost of their own. Every relationship is born of compromise; you want to find a solution that you're both happy with.

This will mean that you will have to be flexible; nobody gets 100% of what they want, either in a partner or a relationship. The price of entry in a relationship means giving up some of the things you might want out of it. The point of a relationship is that what you *do* get is so incredible that they make up for the things you'll have to give up in exchange.

However, everyone has absolute "must haves" or expectations, so when you're having the defining the relationship talk, it's important to be up front about what you want. If you are looking for a relationship that is going to lead towards marriage within a certain period of time, it's vital that you say this. Hiding something you want because you're worried it would chase your partner off is going to just cause heartache down the line. Hoping that you can change their mind about it later when they're more invested is even worse. All this will do is ensure that you're going to have an epic and even more brutal break up later on.

If you want or expect something from your ongoing relationship, you have to say so. Not hint at it, not assume that it comes standard — say it flat out as clearly as you possibly can. If you want exclusivity, let her know: "I've done the dating thing. I want a relationship that's about you and me and nobody else." If you want something casual but you're open to something more committed in the future, then say so: "I love what we have together, but I'm not ready for commitment right now. Don't get me wrong, I *do* want to keep seeing you. Right now, though I want to take things day by day and see what comes."

If you're not the sort of person who can do traditional relationships or can't (or won't) do monogamy then you have to be upfront. If you are going to want an open or poly relationship[2], then you absolutely must establish this when you're defining things.

Whatever you do, do *not* browbeat or pressure your partner into accepting your terms. If your must-haves are their hard deal breakers, then there's nothing left to be said, honestly. It's simply a sign that you and they aren't compatible and that trying to force it to happen is only going to make you both miserable. Just as you don't want to be pressured into a relationship you don't want, neither do they. Explain what you want, be willing to compromise where you can… and be willing to walk away if it just isn't going to work.

I realize it can be hard to advocate for your own wants or needs in a relationship when you run the risk of ending the relationship before it even begins. At the same time, however, it's far better to be single and satisfied with your life than to be stuck in a relationship that makes you — or your partner — miserable. Sometimes what you want and what your erstwhile partner wants are anathema to one another. It may suck like a singularity at a vacuum cleaner convention, but the fact of the matter is that you two weren't going to work out. Yeah, you may love that person, but no matter what the songs say, love *ain't* all you need to make a relationship work[3]. If it's becoming clear that you aren't going to be able to find a compromise that works for the both of you, then it's best to end things.

The cleanest break heals the fastest and gives more opportunities to salvage a friendship when you've had time to heal.

Remember: It's An Ongoing Conversation

When it comes to setting the terms of a relationship, one of the classic blunders[4] is to assume that you're only going to talk about the rules of your relationship once. This actually makes the conversation *more* stressful. There's really no pressure quite like feeling that everything about the future of your relationship hinges on this *one* conversation and afterwards, everything is going to be set in stone — permanent and as unalterable than a contract with Satan.[5]

The fact of the matter is, people change and grow over time. What we want or need from a relationship can — and frequently does — change as we do. We discover that we may actually want things that we would've sworn on a stack of Bibles that we had no interest in, while we may find that we no longer require the things that we thought were absolutely vital. Someone who wanted a strictly casual relationship can realize that they're ready to settle down with something more committed. Someone who is in a strictly monogamous relationship may find themselves open to a little outside play after they've established a common bond of trust and security, while someone in an open relationship may want to close theirs for a while. Somebody who thought she was interested in a relationship leading to marriage may realize that a lifelong commitment isn't for her after all.

This is why it's important to not treat the DTR conversation as a one-and-done event. Instead, go into it understanding that it is an ongoing conversation and something you may come back to many times over the years. This gives your relationship the room and flexibility to grow and change along with the two of you. Being willing to admit that the relationship you have now may not be the relationship you will want years down the line isn't a condemnation of your love or an indication that your relationship is in any way defective or inferior.

And don't forget: it's *your* relationship. Other people don't get to decide the rules of how your relationship works. Relationships aren't open to public vote. It's *all* strictly about what works for the two of you. This means you get to define your relationship as whatever makes you both happy... even if you both decide to toss the rules out and start over from scratch.

---

[1] In fact, as a general rule, it's better not to make promises when either of you are naked...

[2] Note: this can actually change over time. You may not want an open relationship at first but decide you're interested in one later on.

That being said, if you know *now* that you will want a non-monogamous relationship eventually, then it's important to make it clear that this is something you will be coming back to down the line.

[3] Good thing too, otherwise I'd be out of a job. Wait, shit, how do I delete this?

[4] The most famous of which is misunderstanding "No I'm not mad" as being the literal truth, but only slightly less well known is this...

[5] At the other end of the spectrum, admittedly are people who feel free to decide that it doesn't matter what you'd agreed to. "I've altered the terms of our agreement; pray I don't alter them further," is not the sign of future happiness.

THREE

FIVE CONVERSATIONS YOU MUST HAVE

How well do you know your partner?

IF YOU WANT your relationship to go the distance — however long that may be — then the best thing you can do is to lay the groundwork for success well in advance. The key to this is very simple: you make sure that the two of you have the same expectations and understandings when it comes to your relationship... preferably before the two of you get serious.

If you're wondering what I mean, then simply ask yourself: how well do you know your partner? Oh sure, you're reasonably sure that she's not secretly a Deep One or that he's not an intelligent tapeworm wearing that body like a flesh-suit... but how well do you sync on the make-or-break issues? Are the two of you absolutely, 100% sure that your opinions line up on, say, abortion? Or what happens if one or the other of you happens to contract a sexually transmitted infection? What do you consider cheating?

If you're like most couples, you may not actually know. Many couples are very quick to assume that they're on the same page regarding major relationship issues without ever actually talking about them. In fact, many couples get actively uncomfortable having frank conversations about various hypotheticals that may affect you during your life together. Communication is key to a relationship's success, but it only helps if you're communicating about the things that matter. It's completely understandable. It can be unpleasant to talk about worst-case scenarios or to put your sexual cards on the table and wait to see how your partner responds. But as awkward as some of these conversations can be, they're incredibly important.

After all, there's never a worse time to find out that you and your partner don't feel the same way than when you're facing major life events without ever having gamed out how you will respond to them. What might be a minor issue to you may well be a relationship extinction-level event to them and vice-versa, and you don't want to find this just in time to watch your years together go down the drain.

Instead, you want to have these 5 conversations as soon as is reasonably possible when your relationship starts to get serious. You may not be in perfect sync with one another, but simply being able to talk about these issues — when they're still an abstract instead of a very real issue — can make the difference between a relationship for the ages and an ugly break-up.

Keep in mind: while it's important to have these conversations early, it should be noted that they should be *ongoing* conversations. Circumstances change with time, and so do opinions. What may be unthinkable at one point in your life may be desirable at another, while what may seem obvious when it's theoretical may be much murkier when you're actually dealing with it. By keeping those lines of communication open, you empower yourselves to change and grow together and adapt as need be.

Conversation #1: What Is Your Fighting Style?

No matter how in love the two of you may be, being in a relationship is like the first night of Fight Club: you're *going* to fight. Yes, your partner is absolutely perfect and the two of you couldn't be any closer without co-starring in *The Human Centipede 3*. Doesn't matter; at some point they're going to say or do something that's just going to piss you right the hell off. And when that happens, you may end up making that inevitable fight worse than it needs to be.

See, everyone has their own way of handling interpersonal conflicts that feels perfectly natural to them. However, what may be incredibly obvious to you may be sending completely different signals to your partner. For example, you may do something I suggest in chapter 8 and make a point of walking off your anger before addressing the conflict. After all, you want a cool and level head so that you don't say something by accident that you will regret later. Your partner, on the other hand, has no idea that this is part of your personal routine; *they* think that by walking away instead of handling things right then and there, you're disrespecting them by implying that you don't *care*.

As a result, what started as a minor disagreement has mutated into the emotional equivalent of Krakatoa.

But let's take a different, surprisingly common scenario. Let's say that you're someone who tears up easily. Your default physical reaction to high levels of emotion — any emotion — brings tears to your eyes. To you, this is just how you are; you're not actually crying, it's just how you're wired. To your partner however, it may represent something completely different; they may see it as you being much more upset than you actually are.

Alternately, they might feel like you're emotionally blackmailing them into giving you what you want, because arguing with someone who's crying makes you the asshole in that situation. As a result: they feel like they can't actually discuss this issue without your trying to (unfairly) shut things down and ends up growing more resentful.

Perhaps you or your partner get loud and excitable when you fight. You don't mean anything by it. It's simply part of the dynamic in your family, how you clear the air with one another. The fight burns bright but as soon as it's over, it's forgotten like it never happened. To someone who's unused to this pattern or fighting style, it may be incredibly intimidating. Or maybe you're someone who gets quieter and more terse when they get angry and your partner doesn't realize that this is a danger sign.

What can make things worse is that sometimes the way two people try to resolve a conflict can have the exact opposite effect – your style is to discuss the issue until you've covered every angle while your partner would rather just find a solution and let it go. All you're trying to do is make sure you understand things; to *them*, it feels like you won't drop the subject and now you're just badgering them to the point of rage . Sure, you both want the same things – you just want to settle the issue so you can both move on – but your styles are so out of sync that you keep poking the emotional bear until it suddenly drops 500 pounds of *FUCK THIS SHIT* all over the relationship.

This is why in the early days of your relationship, you want to explain how you fight, what's going to calm you down and what's only going to make you even angrier. Yes, this means having a level of self-awareness that many people don't have. Fine – start developing it. If you don't, every fight is going to go about as well as juggling bottles of nitroglycerine – you may keep things moving, but it only takes one mistake to blow everything straight to hell.

Conversation #2: How Do You Feel About Sex?

Sexual compatibility is one of the most important parts of a relationship. This goes beyond simply having the right combination of genitals to smash rhythmically together and deep into areas of libido, desired frequency, fantasies, kinks, the kind of sex they *want* to have, the kind that they'll put up with for now and the little things that will make you curl up in the shower. However, most people never realize that they're incompatible until it's too late. We rarely have any conversation about sex – especially early on – where the answer isn't "yes, have some".

It's easy to mistake passion at the beginning of the relationship for long-term compatibility when the novelty of this new partner is drowning your brain in dopamine and you're throwing each other up against any flat surface in the house.

Unfortunately, the honeymoon period *always* comes to an end and that's a bad time to find out that you have conflicting ideas about what "good sex" means.

To give one common example: many people enter into relationships not realizing that they have radically mismatched libidos. It was ok in the beginning, but while you want it every day and twice on Sundays, they're happy with once a month or less. Worse, they discover that their partner has single-handedly decided that at some point in the future, they're going to be done with having sex… but still expect exclusivity.

Some people may have kinks that they were able to ignore in the early days but they won't ultimately be satisfied if they can't indulge them. Other people are incredibly vanilla[1] and get squicked out by any sort of non-traditional sex-practices. This doesn't mean that one partner is better or more evolved than the other; it simply means that they may well be completely incompatible in the long-term.

When you're starting to get serious, it's important to lay your cards on the table: are there sexual needs that you *must* have met in order to be satisfied? Are you willing to explore some sexual interests (within reason) you don't share in the name of being a good, giving and game partner? If your partner has interests or fetishes that you can't or won't fulfill, are you ok with them getting those needs met elsewhere?

You also want to establish how you feel about sex in the long-term. One depressingly common problem in relationships is the tendency for society to treat commitment or marriage as the death of sexual adventure. For many people, wild, crazy, swinging-from-the-chandelier sex is for when you're young and fancy-free; once you've settled down, it's time to put the spreader-bar and hand-cuffs away and quit finding people for threesomes, foursomes and moresomes.

Once you dispose of these preconceived notions about committed sex vs. the sex you have when you're single , committed relationships are perhaps the *best* time to explore sex more — after all, part of the point of a commitment is increasing levels of trust and openness with your partner. However, many people, even in long-term relationships often have a hard time opening up to their partners about their fantasies; they fear — sometimes with reason — that their partners would react badly to their *real* fantasies. I've known many people of all genders who answered the question "What's your fantasy?" with perfect honesty, only to have their partners freak out. As a result, they're punished twice: first for having the fantasy and again for being honest about it.

Small wonder they may get increasingly gun-shy about talking about their real desires the longer the relationship goes on.

What makes it even sadder is that sometimes they become convinced that their fantasy is so dark or taboo, despite it actually being decidedly tame. But because they never have this conversation, they believe that they can't possibly explore their kink with their partner... because how could anyone respect someone who wanted to get spanked?

It's important to establish those open lines of communication early and build the trust and open-mindedness necessary for an honest discussion about your feelings about sex. It can be difficult — we worry about what our partners will think if our interests are at all unconventional. However as awkward as it might be at first, it does get easier the more you do it. The more you get in the habit of communicating with your partner, the more it becomes a natural part of your relationship.

Plus, if your partner is going to react badly when your deepest fantasy involves cuckolding or being tied to a Saint Andrew's Cross and have hot wax poured on your squishy bits, it's better to find this out early on rather than years down the line.

Conversation #3: Are You On The Same Page About Monogamy?

Some conversations are important to have because it's entirely too easy to assume they're not necessary. The cruel irony of this is that these assumptions mean they're more important than ever. In western culture, particularly in the United States, monogamy is considered the default for relationships. It's just assumed that if you're entering into a committed relationship, you're signing on for sexual and romantic exclusivity.

However, the fact that it's the standard option, culturally, doesn't automatically mean that this is what everybody actually wants. And in fact, many cultural assumptions about monogamy actually can make maintaining a monogamous commitment *harder*.

As I said in chapter 1, the narrative of monogamy is that it's effortless and natural. Every classic love story tells us that once you're in love with someone, you'll never want anyone else. And while that may be true for some people, it's not true for everyone. I've lost track of how many letters I've received from people in otherwise happy relationships who are terrified because they suddenly find themselves t w i t t e r p a t e d   o v e r   s o m e o n e   e l s e.   T o   t h e m ,   t h i s sudden, harmless infatuation goes from pants-tightening day-dreams and giggly energy to a source of needless anxiety and despair.

Monogamy simply means making a promise to your partner that you're not going to have sex with someone else. It doesn't mean that you won't *want* to sleep with other people.[2]

Some people are very good at monogamy. Many people aren't, and trying to make a monogamous commitment is setting themselves up for an inevitable failure. There are people for whom monogamy simply doesn't work; they may be polyamorous, they may want or need many partners across the gender spectrum or they simply be unable to restrict themselves to having sex with only one person for extended periods of time. This doesn't make them bad people, just people who don't fit into a very specific, very narrow cultural construct.

Despite the assumption that monogamy comes standard, it's important to talk honestly about monogamy and sexual fidelity, especially if you or your partner have cheated before. It's an understandably difficult conversation to have – there's a lot of social pressure to go with the flow and just say that you're monogamous. People who don't are frequently labeled as sluts, dogs, selfish or simply weak-willed. They're told that there's something wrong with them and that their desires are wrong. And there's the very legitimate worry that if you're honest, your partner may reject you because he or she doesn't feel the same way.

But as with conversations about sexual preferences, it's a conversation that's important to have early on. If you know that you can't do traditional monogamy, then it's important to let your partner know early on so that they can make an informed decision about the future of your relationship. Even if you're both on the same page, being able to talk openly and sincerely about your expectations and needs with regards to sexual fidelity is important because of how it makes future conversations easier. People can and do change their minds over time – what might be unthinkable at one stage in your relationship may be possible, even exciting later on… once you've built up greater levels of trust and emotional commitment to one another. But even if you or your partner aren't likely to change your minds on the matter, being able to actually talk about the issue without fear of rejection or judgement is a cornerstone of a successful relationship.

And as long as we're talking about incredibly difficult conversations….

Conversation #4: What Happens if Somebody Cheats?

This conversation is one of the hardest to have with a partner because, frankly, it's one of the most loaded topics you can bring up in a relationship. But at as much as you might want to close your eyes and assume that it won't be an issue, it's important to face it head on.

The fact of the matter is: Infidelity happens. It's difficult to say how frequently because, frankly, people are motivated to lie about cheating when self-reporting in studies – even under terms of strict anonymity. However, the most reliable studies suggest that up to 20% of men and 15% of women under 35 have been unfaithful in their relationship[3], while others suggest that nearly a quarter of men and a fifth of women are likely to stray[4]. And as gender roles change and women become more secure financially,   the infidelity gap between men and women is closing rapidly.[5]

There's no question that cheating on your partner is a shitty thing to do. In a perfect world, people in monogamous relationships wouldn't cheat, and the ones who do would own up to it, giving their partner a chance to get tested and treated if need be. But we don't live in a perfect world, nor are we perfect people. Not every cheater is a mustache twirling villain or a self-involved prick; more often than not, they're just all-too human. Establishing a plan of action in the event of an infidelity can save a great deal of heart-ache up front, as well as hopefully avoiding damage to a person's health.

As much as many may debate whether cheating can be the lesser of two (or more) evils, it's inevitably a betrayal of trust and one that causes no small amount of pain. For many people, cheating is automatically an relationship extinction-level event… but this attitude can actually end up doing more damage in the long run than the actual affair.

Treating infidelity as a one-size-fits-all crime ignores the realities and difficulties of a monogamous commitment. Very, very few people are able to exercise monogamy perfectly and mistakes will happen. A singular slip-up under unusual circumstances isn't the same as someone maliciously abusing another person's trust; treating them as equal is needlessly draconian. Relationships can be repaired – even made stronger than before if both parties are willing to work on the issues that lead up to the infidelity.

To start with, deciding that cheating automatically means ending the relationship may well mean throwing away a relationship that is potentially salvageable. As tempting as it is to portray a cheater as selfish and evil and out to destroy the relationship, affairs are rarely black-and-white issues. We tend to get caught up in a number of myths surrounding infidelity that color our response to a partner stepping out on us and what it all means. The fact of the matter is that people cheat for a multitude of reasons. Sometimes cheating is a way of slamming one's hand down on the Relationship Self-Destruct button. Sometimes it's a one-time event in a moment of weakness that's unlikely to ever happen again. Sometimes it's a response to circumstances within the relationship. And yes, sometimes they're just an asshole who wants to get theirs and couldn't care less about who it hurts in the process.

However the most frequent — and dangerous — side-effect of treating infidelity as an automatic relationship ender is that it actually can endanger the other partner's health. Sex carries risks and one of those risks is for sexually transmitted infections. While condoms do provide protection against STIs, they aren't 100% even in perfect use... and many people – up to 50% – don't use them consistently or correctly[6]. Moreover, the vast majority of the population don't use condoms or dental dams for oral sex, which can *also* spread STI's. By treating infidelity as an automatic relationship-ender, the cheating partner is incentivized to not disclose his straying and any potential consequences... which leaves the other partner ignorant of the possibility that they may well have been infected themselves. By having a plan of action — a relationship "worst case scenario" plan, as it were — you will at least have created the circumstances under which the two of you can resolve the issue without needlessly endangering someone else's physical health along with their emotional well-being.

Don't get me wrong: finding out that your partner cheated on you is almost always a gut-punch. Having this conversation — a willingness to discuss potential problems in the relationship and agreeing on how to handle them in advance — won't make your relationship immune to potential infidelities. Deciding if the relationship is salvageable and how best to save it, is difficult and emotionally taxing.   It may well still end with kicking your partner's ass to the curb. But having this conversation may give you both the tools to overcome what – in the long run – will be a rough patch in an otherwise glorious relationship.

Conversation #5: What Happens If We Get Pregnant?

Remember what I said about sex carrying risks? An unintended pregnancy is the ultimate risk for sexual activity.

Unless you're sterilized, committed to exclusively non-procreative sex acts[7] or are in a same-sex relationship, there is always the risk of pregnancy. Most contraception is incredibly effective under *perfect* use. The problem is that perfect use rarely resembles *typical* use. Condoms break or slip off[8], IUDs shift out of place[9], hormonal birth control's effectiveness can vary depending on a multitude of factors, including body weight[10] and the Morning After pill is frequently less effective than other forms of contraception.[11] Even layering contraceptive methods isn't proof against an unintended pregnancy; the odds are drastically lowered, but they still are not zero.

The likelihood that you and your partner will get pregnant may be incredibly remote, but shit can and does happen.

That's why it's important that you be able to talk about what you are both willing to do in the event that it does.

Handling an unintended pregnancy is an incredibly stressful, potentially life-altering event and it's vitally important that the two of you are on the same page. It's frequently a difficult conversation to have when it's a thought-exercise; it's even harder to have when it's gone from "theoretical" to "actually happening oh god oh god oh god." It's also an area where you're likely to step on landmines that you may not realize are there if the two of you haven't actually discussed the possibility of pregnancy before. After all, calling abortion a divisive issue is rather like describing Fat Man and Little Boy as overpowered firecrackers. Finding out that your partner's views are diametrically opposed to yours in the middle of a pregnancy scare is a great way to turn a stressful situation into a goddamned nightmare.

Talking about handling a potential pregnancy goes beyond just whether you're both in favor of abortion or not or whether you'll put the child up for adoption. You should discuss in advance what sorts of contraception you want to use and when, instead of just assuming that one of you will be responsible for it. There are a number of factors that play into which contraception methods are right for both of you, including cost, insurance coverage, availability and potential side-effects. This is especially true over the course of a long-term relationship, when your contraception needs may change over time.

You should also discuss whether you're willing (or able) to have children now or further down the line or if you want to have children at all. If you are both sure that you don't want children, then you need to discuss whether you'll employ a more permanent form of contraception such as a vasectomy, a tubal ligation or a tubal occlusion.

The cold hard truth is that handling an unintended pregnancy has potential consequences – life-long consequences – for both of you; if you aren't on the same page, you need to not be fucking.

[1] Incidentally, I really dislike this term for people who aren't into kink; unfortunately, I have yet to find one that isn't *more* problematic.

[2] And for the record: fantasies aren't cheating. Rubbing one out to someone you're not dating isn't cheating. Whatever goes on between your ears and behind your eyes is your own business.

[3] http://www.nytimes.com/2008/10/28/health/28well.html?_r=1

[4] http://www.livescience.com/14671-cheating-personality.html

[5] http://www.bloomberg.com/news/articles/2013-07-02/cheating-wives-narrowed-infidelity-gap-over-two-decades

[6] http://www.nbcnews.com/health/health-news/condom-use-101-basic-errors-are-so-common-study-finds-f207925

[7] So, anal sex, oral sex, mutual masturbation, frottage or other forms of sex-play that don't run the risk of sperm coming in contact with eggs.

[8] http://www.ncbi.nlm.nih.gov/pubmed/8070546

[9] https://www.verywell.com/how-to-check-your-iud-strings-906659

[10] http://www.cdc.gov/reproductivehealth/unintendedpregnancy/contraception.htm

[11] http://www.webmd.com/sex/birth-control/plan-b

Four

HOW TO COMMUNICATE THE RIGHT WAY

"What We've Got Here is... Failure To Communicate."

ONE OF THE most important skills when it comes to relationship maintenance is communication. However, there's a difference between "communication" and "filling the air with noise". The fact that you're talking doesn't mean that you're actually being understood, and the fact that you can hear someone doesn't mean that you're actually *listening*. As much as we're taught that communication is the key to solving all of a relationship's problems, it remains one of those areas where couples have *vastly* different ideas of what communication does and doesn't mean.

All the talking in the world doesn't mean a damned thing if one person see's their honey-bunny's lips moving but all they hear is "wa wa wa wa wa wa" like a bizarrely sexual version of Charlie Brown's teacher.

Whether you want to increase the intimacy in your relationship, find ways of getting closer with your honey or simply find more effective ways of clearing the air, you want to make sure that you're not just heard but understood. And that means making sure you're communicating the *right* way.

Understand Your Communication Style (and Learn Your Partner's)

Let's start with one of the biggest issues when it comes to the way that couples miscommunicate. For many couples, the problem isn't that they're not communicating it's that they're communicating in a way that their partner doesn't understand. This goes beyond gendered "Men are From Mars, Women are From A Different Cliché" bullshit and straight into functionally speaking different Languages

Everybody has their own personality quirks that dictate the way we try to get our message to other people. However, we *also* tend to assume that our personal quirks are completely clear and understandable to others — or that they're simply *universal*. It's one thing when you're with your friends or family, people who've had years to learn your particular idiosyncrasies and adapt accordingly. In most cases, your partner *hasn't*, especially at the beginning of the relationship. Thus, despite your best intentions, communication gets thwarted, feelings get hurt and nobody understands what's happening and why.

You think you're making yourself perfectly clear. Your partner, on the other hand, is mystified like a dog that doesn't understand why the cat doesn't want to be his friend.

One of the most common examples of conflicting communication styles is the classic "women want sympathy/ men want solutions" dichotomy. Because of differences in how men and women are socialized, they frequently bump heads during times of conflict. Women are frequently socialized to commiserate and empathize when their friends complain; complaints are about venting frustrations and seeking reassurance. Men, on the other hand, are taught that a friend complaining or griping means that the person is asking for a solution to the problem at hand. When there's no attempt to bridge the gap, it can lead to frustration on both sides — men feeling like their suggestions are being ignored while women are feeling like their partner isn't listening to them.

Other times, it may be that you think that what you're doing is an unmistakable sign of your affection and appreciation for your partner. To *them*, however, it's "the things we do on alternate Tuesdays". You think you're signaling that you want sex when you start rubbing your girlfriend's shoulders; meanwhile, your girlfriend thinks that you're just being nice to her after she's had a long and aggravating day at work and sex is the *last* thing on her mind. Now she thinks that the back rub came with strings attached while you're not sure why she's getting upset with you for wanting to move things into the bedroom. You *think* you're speaking the same language but coming away with completely different meanings and it's leaving everybody frustrated and annoyed.

Occasionally it's a matter of differences in personality. Some people are perpetually jokey and playful and will use humor to diffuse tense situations that make them uncomfortable. Other people consider certain topics to be too important to be joked about and find those tension-breaking jokes to be a sign of disrespect. It's not a matter of one person being right and the other being wrong, but simply how they relate to the issue at hand.

Some people hold everything in and only open up when they

reach a boiling point, while others let it all hang out with the enthusiasm of a family Thanksgiving free-for-all after cracking open the fourth bottle of wine. Some people, especially when dealing with emotional or complex relationship topics, will prefer to take time to formulate their thoughts so they can express themselves clearly. Meanwhile, their partners may see their unwillingness to address the problem right then and there to be a sign of not respecting them enough to give an answer or to take the topic seriously.

Misunderstanding your partner's communication style can lead to, well, profound miscommunications. As I mentioned earlier, there are people who start to tear up when they get worked up emotionally. *Any* emotions — happiness, sadness, the triumph of cooking especially tasty pasta fagioli, whatever — makes them start to cry like they just saw an Sarah McLaughlin ASPCA commercial. Their partners, on the other hand, can't stand it; they see the tears well up and assume that it's a way of shutting the conversation down because what kind of insensitive bastard keeps going after he's made his boyfriend cry?

Part of effective communication in a relationship is learning how to adapt your communication style to your partner's and how to translate your partner's communication style to your own. Responding to "sex?" with "WAFFLE IRONS!" is only going to leave everyone confused and vaguely hungry.

(Well, assuming you're not a pair of Dadaists anyway…)

But speaking of being misunderstood…

Quit Assuming You're A Mind Reader

A lot of people, even people in long-term relationships, make the mistake of believing that they know their partner's position on everything. While it's true that over time you get a pretty good handle on your partner's likes, dislikes, pet-peeves and peccadillos[1], it's not a guarantee that you actually know how they feel about a particular topic. When you assume you know how they feel already, you tend to end up reacting to the assumption you've assigned to them in your head, rather than how they really feel.

I've lost track of how many people have had more crises than the DC Universe[2] because they had an issue they didn't *dare* bring up to their partner. In their minds, they had already had this discussion this discussion a thousand times, knew *exactly* how it would turn out and there was just no point in actually trying to talk it out in person. However, because they've already decided how things would play out, they're starting to respond as though they've actually *had* the argument. Now, maybe they're right; maybe it would go badly. Maybe they're completely wrong. But because they're responding to what they *assume* is their partner's position, they've begun to get angry and resent the disagreement they haven't actually *had*. This in turn leads to other, *real*, conflicts.

Assuming that you already have the answer before you've actually brought up the topic is a great way to borrow trouble from a future that may never actually come to pass. Not only do you end up with the emotional fallout from the fight, but the inciting incident never gets resolved. Hell, your partner may not realize that there's a problem in the first place because you won't bring it up. As a result: the problem continues unabated while you get angry that a) there's a problem and b) you had an imaginary fight about it.

Yes, you may know your partner well, but you're not a mind-reader. Until you've actually sat down and talked things out, you have no idea if your girlfriend's position on, say, mangosteens, has changed. Perhaps she's willing to give them a try now. Maybe she's had other issues around tropical fruit that meant she was rejecting them out of hand but deep down she'd always been curious about them and is finally in a place to actually experiment with them a little[3].

Ahem. That got away from me a little.

Anyway.

This tendency to respond to the assumption versus the reality often goes both ways; it's entirely possible that your partner has something that they're afraid to bring up because they believe they know how you'll react – especially if the topic is one that *you* had a strong negative reaction to in the past. It's not unreasonable to conclude that the position someone held two months ago, six months ago, or two years ago hasn't changed, but it's still better to talk things out rather than just presume.

Avoiding assumptions and presumptions about how your partner feels means being willing to bring up possibly difficult topics and actively listening to what they have to say... and making sure you understand. Ask questions. Repeat their position as *you* understand it to be, just to make sure you're clear. Make sure you get *why* they feel that way, not just that they do.

Sometimes the issue isn't the act or the situation or what-not, it's the issues behind them.

As long as we're on the topic of bringing up difficult topics and uncomfortable conversations...

Take Your Parnter Seriously

You know what's a great way to ensure that your partner never reaches out to you with something they feel strongly about? Treat it as though it was something absurd.

Part of what makes being in a relationship work is being able to be open and honest with your partner – even to make yourself deliberately vulnerable to them. Even in a long term, committed relationship, it can take a lot of courage for someone to open up to a partner. If it's a topic that they might be sensitive over, then just bringing it up can be pants-shittingly terrifying.

They might be hesitant to bring up something that's bothering them because they're afraid of how you'll react. They may try afraid to initiate a conversation about a desire they have because they worry that you're going to judge them for having it in the first place. They might be trying to share a goal, a dream, even some hope for the future because for the first time, they feel secure enough with somebody to actually open up and share this incredibly intimate part of themselves.

They are exposing some sensitive and delicate part of themselves, an especially vulnerable spot in their psyche, because they believe that they can trust you with it. It is one moment that can completely redefine the future of your relationship together. And if you treat them like they're being ridiculous or childish or disgusting or just reacts dismissively out of hand, they learn not to share any more. They close in around themselves. What's the point of opening up to your partner when you're just going to get smacked down for it?

Treating your partner's desires or concerns as something unimportant — or worse, just stupid — is a great way to gut-shoot a relationship; it may not die right away, but you've definitely set it on the path to a long, slow and torturous ending. Diminishing someone's insecurities, insulting their needs or desires, telling someone they're being childish or stupid or that they don't have a right to feel the way they do is an indication of how you feel about them as a person.

Don't get me wrong: this doesn't mean that everything must be treated with the reverence of a papal bull, nor does it mean that you need to agree with them on all things. But it *is* important to hear your partner out and to give them the respect of actually listening and paying attention to what they have to say. It may be silly to you, but it's clearly serious to them... otherwise they wouldn't be bringing it up in the first place.

Some Fights Need To Happen

Another thing I see people do that inadvertently shuts down communication between couples: they try to be too "safe". They get caught up in the idea that fights are inherently bad and so they take steps to avoid them at all costs. They believe that the fewer arguments you have in a relationship, the better (or more mature or what-have-you) the relationship is because it means that the two of you are just *that* in synch with one another. So they avoid controversial topics. They "agree to disagree" whenever a subject becomes too heated. They try to put out verbal fires before they even start.

It's a noble idea, one that arises out of the best of intentions: minimizing conflict in a relationship. It also means that at some point, their relationship is going to explode like Vesuvius in the middle of an Olive Garden.

I'm not going to lie: as soon as somebody tells me that they never fight or stop fights before they happen, I mentally start the countdown clock to their incredibly ugly break-up. While it's a good idea to handle disagreements and relationship conflicts in a calm and mature manner, trying to squash any possible disagreements or friction can actually end up making things worse in the long run. When the goal becomes avoiding the fight or heading the conflict off at the pass, then often very little actually gets resolved; it becomes a matter of prizing the calm surface and ignoring the currents raging underneath.

This is, in many ways, the opposite of communication. You may be talking, but you're shutting down a dialogue that you may need to be having.

Think of it like forest fires. As dangerous as they are, some fires are actually necessary for the forest's ecology; they're critical for habitat renewal and prevent the buildup of flammable debris. By focusing exclusively on wildfire suppression, you actually end up making things worse. Not only preventing revitalization of the region but increasing the risk of larger, far more dangerous fires that can devastate an area beyond repair.

Sort of like relationships, really.

To extend an awkward metaphor a little further: when couples try to stamp out sparks before they can catch and flare up, you frequently miss the smoldering embers that are creating the sparks in the first place. You may have stopped *this* fight, but you've just ensured that the explosion later is going to be that much more epic and dramatic.

Sometimes you need to let the argument actually happen so that you can get past the surface issues and down to the core, where the real problem is and get to resolving things after the fighting's over.

Not All Communication is Verbal

"We never talk," is often heralded as a sign of problems within a relationship. Long and involved conversations are held up as the *ne plus ultra* of communication and building rapport; people who aren't very verbal or are more withdrawn are seen as somehow being deficient.

Somebody who isn't willing to open up and share their feelings is seen as holding back and being an impediment to intimacy. The desire for reciprocity becomes mandatory – one partner has opened up and spilled out their feelings, so now the other needs to do so as well, because reasons.

In many ways, there's an unspoken threat in the demand for this equivalent exchange: if you don't open up just as much as your partner did, then you're doing something wrong, committing an emotional crime of sorts. The partner who's just verbalized how they feel is left out in the cold, standing there with their metaphorical dick in their hand. Moreover, you have to do reciprocate to the exact same extent and volume as your partner did because obviously you want things to be equal right?

One of the more well-known examples of this in pop-culture is the movie *Ghost*. One of the defining aspects of Sam (played by Patrick Swayze) and Molly's (played by Demi Moore) relationship is that Sam never says "I love you", he says "ditto". The film portrays this as a defect on Sam's part — he's clearly afraid of intimacy because he won't just say the stupid words. There's the implication that Molly can't *really* know that Sam loves her because, well, he didn't *say* it. That assumption — that it's not real unless you actually say the words — is all over the place in our culture. If somebody isn't willing to verbalize how they feel, then by God that's a flaw that needs to be addressed![4]

But while talking is important, it's not the *only* form of communication, nor is it the only way to express oneself. Not everybody is verbally expressive. Prioritizing words over deeds often means overlooking or devaluing the way that individuals *do* express themselves. The person who isn't big on saying "I love you" but shares your bed, takes care of you, cooks for you, holds you when you're upset and makes a point of doing little things that they know you appreciate just because, is saying that they love you just as loudly and declaratively as someone who writes an epic poem on the subject.

So much of communication is non-verbal, yet it seems odd to put the most meaning on words instead of actions. After all, when a person's words conflict with their actions, we assume that the truth is in how they behave rather than in what they say... yet somehow this doesn't hold as true when it comes to communicating within the relationship. Sometimes it's easier to *show* how you feel rather than to say it.

Your partner may not necessarily be using their words, but that doesn't mean that they aren't trying to communicate with you. Part of successful communication in a relationship isn't in what you say, it's in making the effort to understand what your partner is saying... no matter how they're doing it.

---

[1] One typo while entering "sexual peccadillos" into Google lead to a very confusing, yet spicy, rabbit hole, let me tell you...

[2] If you understood this, then I'm so, so sorry.

[3] We... we aren't talking about fruit any more are we?

[4] While not being verbally expressive isn't the worst thing in the world, it *can* lead to other related issues. More on that later.

FIVE

THE IMPORTANCE OF BOUNDARIES

Strong Boundaries Make For A Strong Relationship

ONE IMPORTANT FACTOR in having a happy, successful relationship that rarely gets brought up is to have strong boundaries. At the same time however, it can be surprisingly difficult to *enforce* those boundaries within a relationship.

It's one thing when you're trying to enforce your boundaries against, say, your co-workers who try to take advantage of your generous nature or toxic "friends" who smile while they slide the dagger home into your self-esteem. It's easy to cast others as users, parasites or emotional vampires who prey on people with weak boundaries.

It's another entirely when you're trying to enforce them against someone who shares your life and your bed. Someone who you love and who loves you. Someone who you trust with your heart, your soul and your HBO Go password. Especially if you haven't had strong boundaries up until now. But even within the happiest relationship, it's important to have your boundaries. Just because you let somebody into your life doesn't mean that you don't have a life or desires of your own, or that they may not pressure you into compliance. Ideally, having strong boundaries have kept the users and abusers out of your life. But sometimes they slip through. Other times, people may not realize that their behavior encroaches on your emotional space. They may not be *intentionally* malicious; they're just "strong personalities" who are used to "getting their way," without considering how it affects others.

And sometimes you're just dealing with people who were willing to keep their real nature in check until they felt more in control and were ready to start exerting control over you. Sometimes it's overt, sometimes it's subtle, but the end result is the same: they get what they want out of you and you end up feeling worse than ever before.

Knowing your limits, what you're willing to put up with and being willing to stand up for yourself is your filter. It will push out the toxic people in your life and help strengthen and drama-proof an otherwise healthy relationship.

Remember: having boundaries isn't rudeness, it's self-defense.

Your Boundaries Are Not A Democracy

One of the first things you need to realize: you and you alone decide where you set your boundaries. Even within the bounds of a relationship, your boundaries are strictly up to you. Dating someone, having children with them or marrying them doesn't mean that you no longer have autonomy over your life and where you set your limits. This can actually be a difficult step for a lot of people — especially if you didn't have strong boundaries to begin with.

If you're not a naturally assertive person, there's a tendency to not want to rock the boat or make people needlessly upset. You get used to the idea of "going along to get along", because you'd really rather not cause a fuss or trigger a confrontation. Even if you are more self-assured, you may not want to pick a fight with those particular people for a multitude of reasons.

Thing is? People who trade on pushing other people's boundaries recognize this and will cheerfully exploit that tendency. Even people who aren't actively evil or assholish will push against the idea that you're wrong for deciding where to draw the line.

What you need to keep in mind is that people who trade on your weak boundaries — both the toxic and the merely selfish — aren't going to present themselves like cartoon villains. They're not going to be twirling their mustaches at you and cackling madly as they tell you that you're not allowed to say what you are or aren't willing to do or be comfortable with. The obvious challenges to your boundaries are fairly self-evident – the ever classic threat of "if you don't do X, I'll do Y." A girlfriend or boyfriend implying that they'd cheat on you or leaving various threats hanging like the Sword of Damocles if you don't give in are classic examples of someone trying to push your boundaries.

The insidious ones are the ones that don't feel like challenges… they're the times when people will pull you aside and say "Come, let us REASON together." They will try to make you feel *bad* about having boundaries and not acceding to their wishes. They're the ones who will try to trade on your guilt ("It's not fair…", "You know how lonely/ jealous I get!") or to implore you to be "reasonable" or be incredulous or hurt that you're "making such a big deal out of this." They'll try to leverage social pressure — the classic "everybody else is doing it!" or "my ex used to do this/ be cool with this" — or complain about how you "used to be cool/fun/not like this" when trying to get you to let them walk all over you or assign you responsibilities that aren't yours.

But at the end of the day, their opinions don't matter. Your choices aren't up for a public vote. Other people don't get to approve or veto your decisions. People can think what they want, but they don't get a say unless you choose to give them one. You and you alone have the exclusive right to decide what you will and won't put up with and where you will set your boundaries.

If you decide that you, say, have a hard line against any sort of sexual activity before marriage, that's your choice. It's a choice that other people may disagree with or think is a bad idea, but it's still *your* choice and your right to decide that this is what you want. Similarly, if you decide to relax your boundaries for one person or one group – for whatever reason you may have – that's your choice as well; you're not obligated to be "fair" or give other people "the same chance". It's well within your rights to have boundaries in one place for family members and another for your partner. You can even adjust your boundaries over time if you choose. You can be as arbitrary as you please, if that's what you really want. And if you decide that it's not what you want… then you're welcome to move them wherever you please, whenever you please.

But only if it's your choice.

Let me be clear: throwing the word "boundaries" is *not* a get-out-of-jail-free card. People are quite capable of abusing their boundaries as a way of controlling or compelling others. Similarly, having a boundary in one area or another doesn't mean that you are free from responsibility. You're still going to have to deal with the consequences of enforcing those boundaries. But that's part and parcel of the deal: you accept those consequences as the price for having them because they're that important to you.

And while we're talking about people trying to change your mind:

"No" Is A Full Sentence

When you're dealing with someone trying to push against your boundaries — whether they're trying to pressure you into buying things you don't need or volunteer you for things that you don't want to do — there's an almost inevitable temptation to justify your reasons for refusal. You may want to explain why you can't in ways that don't seem as blunt as "I don't want to." You may feel the need to come up with an excuse as to why you won't (not can't, *won't*) do something.

This is actually a mistake. As soon as you're explaining why you can't, you've opened up a chink in your defenses. When you justify or explain your refusal, what you're telling people is that you don't believe that you have the right to refuse in the first place. Instead, you're trying to bolster it with evidence, as though you were proving a case in a court of law. By trying to excuse or justify your refusal, you're tacitly admitting that you *could* be wrong, and people will pounce on this.

You see this all the time in high-pressure sales tactics; when someone goes from flat-out refusing to explaining why they possibly couldn't, they've all but conceded the fight. Once you've started to offer reasons and excuses and justifications, you've lowered your shields and made yourself vulnerable to counter-arguments. Now it's not a refusal, it's a *debate*. Those excuses or reasons you offer will be met by counter-offers or suggestions about how you could do the thing and whatever is keeping you from doing the thing. That, in turn means that you're going to either have to elaborate – at which point, you're justifying yourself to someone and losing emotional ground – or offer rebuttals to something that probably wasn't even true in the first place. And unless you're a very capable liar (or someone who just plain doesn't care) odds are that they know you're just making things up. Then you're going to feel embarrassed and ashamed for lying in the first place and they're going to leverage that against you.

The way you avoid letting someone through your defenses is to not give them that opportunity in the first place. "No," is all you need to say. You don't need to be rude about it – "I'm sorry but I can't," "I'm sorry, no", "No, thank you" and "I appreciate the thought but, no" are all valid ways of politely refusing – but you do need to be firm. Just as other people don't get a say in where you draw your lines, they also don't need to approve of your reasons for refusing. If they ask, then you repeat yourself: "No, I said I can't." Repeat it over and over again if you have to. To the point of absurdity if necessary.

"No" is your brick wall, your force field, your *Thibault* against their *Capa Ferro*. "No" is all that needs to be said.

In terms of a relationship, there *are* times that it's important to explain your refusal. There can be times when your partner may be asking things of you that they don't realize are an issue for you. Explaining your reasoning for something being an issue can help them understand your side of things and help the two of you find some other solution that's more acceptable to you both. However, if they start to try to argue with you *about* your reasons or pressure you into doing things you've ruled off limits *anyway*… that's when the flat "no" comes right back into play. They have demonstrated that they are ignoring your stated wishes and now you're back to defending yourself against their pressure tactics.

Now to be sure: this can be difficult to do. You'll feel uneasy. You'll have to fight against an entirely natural and understandable impulse to soften things and explain. You have to apply your willpower and stick to your guns. "No," is a complete sentence, and it's all you need to say.

Be Willing To Be Break The Social Contract

Part of being willing to maintain your boundaries means being willing to ignore or break the social contract.

The social contract, put simply, is the collection of the unwritten rules that govern our social interactions. For example, just getting up and leaving a conversation without another word is against the social contract; it's rude and moreover, it's weird. So is just walking up and putting your hands on a total stranger. Breaking the social contract marks you as someone who's poorly socially calibrated or who has low emotional intelligence and thus someone to be avoided in polite society.

It's also how people will try to push you into moving your boundaries for them.

There are a number of ways that the social contract gives people influence over one another – various ways that we are obligated to others. One of the most obvious ways — and a way that is frequently abused by toxic people — is the rule of reciprocation. If someone does us a favor — or is *seen* as doing us a favor —then we feel a sense of obligation to repay them with a favor of our own. One of the most obvious examples of this comes from high-pressure sales tactics; by pretending to do somebody a favor, such as offering them a "discount", a salesman creates a sense of obligation to return the favor, even if it's just by continuing to give them the opportunity to pitch to you.

A toxic person intent on pushing your boundaries may do something for you unasked and then use that to push you into agreeing to do something you don't want to do under the guise of "Well, I did this for *you*..." They may even throw the fact that they did something in your face as proof that you're being "unreasonable". Other times, it will take the form of weaponized guilt. Anyone with a toxic parent will recognize the "classic" guilt lines – "all these things I've done for you and you can't do this one thing for me?"

Of course, it can be hard to recognize attempts at manipulation for actual favors. After all, it's not uncommon to do things for your partner just because you think they'd like it or because you want to do something nice for them. It's the implied obligation to reciprocate that's the tell; it's not a favor if it comes with strings attached. Especially if it's something you haven't asked them to do for you.

Other times, they may try to drag you into their drama. They'll insist that you have some sort of responsibility to shoulder their burdens because of your pre-existing relationship, no matter how tenuous. Emotionally abusive partners will use your relationship to them in order to coerce you into agreeing to things that you don't want to do, are uncomfortable with or that aren't your responsibility to handle in the first place. Similarly, toxic friends will coerce you into taking part in something you disapprove of or bailing them out of a situation of their own making because "that's what friends do", using their relationship with you as a form of obligation rather than asking for help.

Still other times they'll simply make you feel bad for refusing. People who've had extra responsibilities dumped on them at work will be familiar with this tactic — they're making such a *minor* request and it's totally unfair of you to say no. Or they may leverage your fear of being rude as a way to get the metaphorical foot in the door; you don't want to be mean, so you're obligated to let them make their pitch or request.

Being willing to maintain your boundaries frequently means that you have to consciously choose to break the contract. You have to ignore the rule of reciprocity or the dictums against rudeness. It's difficult to do; even if you're not conscious of the social contract, it's still been ingrained in you from birth. You're going to naturally fear some sort of nebulous consequence for doing so, whether it's the other person's disappointment or societal judgement for ignoring the unwritten rules. Just as with saying "no" and sticking to it, you have to learn to get comfortable with breaking the social contract when necessary.

You May Break Up Over This. This Is A Good Thing

One of the reasons why people are often hesitant to enforce their boundaries is because they're worried about causing conflicts with their peers. If they were to quit just "going along with it", their friends, girlfriends, partners, coworkers or what-have-you might abandon them.

Good. That's exactly what enforcing your boundaries is supposed to do.

It's almost disturbing how easy it is for a toxic relationship to become your status quo. It's even more disturbing how we'll often want to preserve that status quo, even when we know it's a bad scene. Humans are adaptable creatures; we can get used to almost anything. And once you're used to something, it's hard to imagine life without it, even when it's *bad* for you. Giving it up means venturing into the unknown. Toxic and abusive people know this and they rely on it. They hold you hostage to your fear of change in order to get you to lower your guard and ease your boundaries. Emotionally abusive partners are especially prone at holding the threat of a break-up over you and what that would mean. They will attack your self-esteem and try to make you believe that they're the only person who could love you or "put up with you". They'll frame everything you've done as being rude, selfish or inconsiderate. They suck away your energy, time and soul. They prey upon your fears and damage you. Having strong boundaries and enforcing them drives them out of your life and keeps them from getting a hold on you in the first place.

There will be times when it's hard to stand up for yourself. There will be times when you'll hurt people's feelings. There will be times when you will end up pushing people away from you by having boundaries. But at the same time, you'll be taking responsibility for your own life and choices, not letting other people make you endure theirs as well. And you'll be making sure that the people who are in your life are right for you.

The Difference Between Enforcing Boundaries and Being A Selfish Asshole

It's important to note that there are times when you're not enforcing boundaries so much as being a dick to people. Sometimes refusing to to something is how you enforce your boundaries. And sometimes refusing to do something or to accept responsibility for something is being unreasonable and you're just being an asshole.

So how do you tell the difference?

Ultimately, it's about responsibility, to yourself and to the people in your life. Are you being asked to do things or endure things that you would not otherwise do, or having duties or expectations put to you that are outside of your role?

One example I see distressingly frequently is people who allow their "friends" undue liberties. This often takes the form of letting their friends partners run roughshod over them in ways that leave them feeling hurt or embarrassed or humiliated. Sometimes it's verbal — negging, left-handed compliments and put-downs, even flat out insults and humiliating jokes. Other times it's physical – unwanted groping, cruel pranks, or dragging them into scenes and events that would otherwise put them off. At the same time however, the person being intruded upon feels like they can't speak up for themselves because "it's just a joke" or "they don't mean it," or "it's just how so-and-so is".

These are times where enforcing your boundaries is not just justified but *necessary*; you don't have a responsibility to let people hurt you, insult you or make you feel uncomfortable, no matter what your relationship is with them. Even if they're "just trying to help" or "toughen you up", it's unwanted and it's unacceptable.

Another example is if you're being asked to handle responsibilities that otherwise belong to someone else. Is your partner expecting you to constantly be managing their mood – to make sure that they don't get jealous or lonely or bored or otherwise needing your constant input or presence? Are you being pressured to let things slide that would otherwise be intolerable? Are you finding yourself having to do other people's work, including their *emotional* labor that would otherwise be their responsibility? Are you being asked to sacrifice something, especially something important, for somebody else when it's not something that's part of your everyday role? Are you being asked to cover for somebody else's mistakes that you had no hand in?

Those are all prime examples of when you should be enforcing your boundaries.

On the other hand, if you are neglecting your partner to do your own thing or if you are the one blaming others for things that are otherwise your responsibility? Then you're being selfish.

Are you steadfastly refusing to compromise in areas that are within your realm of control or participate in something where the responsibilities are shared equally? That's not enforcing your boundaries, that's just being a dick.

Like I said before: enforcing your boundaries doesn't give you license to ignore your responsibilities to others, particularly to your partner. It's not the catch-all excuse to get your way no matter what. Compromise and sacrifice are part of being in a relationship; blending your lives together means giving of yourself to them, even in ways that you might otherwise prefer not to.

Just remember: compromise and sacrifice go both ways. When a relationship is all give and no take, then it's a sign that boundaries are being violated... whether it's yours or theirs.

SIX
HOW DO YOU KNOW WHEN IT'S LOVE?

Love Bites

ONE OF THE things I tell my readers and clients is that I've had almost every problem they've had, and usually worse. On occasion, I'll get a letter from my readers that are potent reminder of what *I* was like when I was in my teens.

It wasn't pretty, let me tell you.

I was a classic otaku; I was going through the stage where the only things I wanted to talk about were anime, manga and the fact that I wanted to find The One[1] in the worst way. To paraphrase the ever relevant movie *500 Days of Summer,* I could blame this on an early exposure to sad British pop music and completely misunderstanding St. Elmo's Fire[2]. And in fairness, my experiences at the time validated everything I was feeling. Love was *everywhere.* I didn't just have a crush on a girl in high-school or college, I had a mad, all-consuming fire in my heart for her that meant I couldn't eat or sleep.

Well… sleep, anyway. Eating somehow managed to take care of itself, actually. Especially if it involved potato skins or chicken strips.

Every time I was into a girl, I was in love with her with my entire heart and soul. It was a love that would last *forever*. Poets would break themselves to pieces trying to find the words to encompass the enormity of our love. When we broke up (and we always broke up… usually within a few months of getting together) it was a hideous tragedy that would break my heart into pieces, set them on fire and then piss in the ashes, just for good measure.

Maybe you're shaking your head in familiar dismay. It's something that everybody goes through… and the we all usually have the same realization. I was continually mistaking infatuation and limerence for love and I would let it drive me berserk.

It took my first serious relationship to make me realize that I had absolutely no idea what love really was… and I needed a better handle on this whole "love" business if I didn't want all of my relationships to end in tragedy.

I Want To Know What Love Is

The first question that you need to ask is very simple: why do we keep mistaking other emotions for "love"?

Well… you can kinda blame the French for this one. The Western concept of romantic love comes from the concepts of courtly love and chivalry[3] codified in the 12th century where knights had elaborate and — critically — platonic[4] relationships with the ladies of the court to which they served. Marriage at the time, amongst royalty, anyway, wasn't about love but about property exchange. Marriage were ways that houses would seal alliances and business deals, which meant that many noblewomen were in loveless marriages, often to husbands much older than they were.

Now if you throw in someone who's closer to their age as part of the court and keep them in close proximity with one another, you're going to end up with a lot of people with infatuations on one another that couldn't be consummated because of a very strict sense of etiquette (and rather harsh punishments for adultery). This actually became something that was actively *encouraged* in part by the culture at the time.   Just as certain popular novels romanticized stalking and abusive relationships, troubadours took the idea of lovers restrained by circumstance and law, unrequited love and the purity of love vs. the coarseness of sex and ran with it.

One of the most famous love stories in history — the story of Lancelot and Guinevere — is based out of the Chivalric tradition and inserted into the legend of King Arthur by Chrétien de Troyes in what would later become the foundation for fanfic writers' head-canons taking over the actual story.[5]

The idea of "true love" being eternal, that love conquers all obstacles, that love is inherently monogamous, that lovers always think about the ones they love, that someone in love can't eat or sleep for being "love-sick" over their crushes… all arise of the concept of courtly love, passed down through pop-culture for centuries. It became the foundation of what we think love is "supposed" to be like and gets regurgitated to us over and over again until we accept it as truth.

The problem of course, is that this concept of "true love" tends to want to ignore things like biology and psychology and often doesn't match up to reality.

It's A Heartbreak Beat

The obvious question at this point is: so what's the problem here?

When you're young, you think you know everything there is to know about… well, everything. You're the first generation to ever feel this way and nobody else can really understaaaaand, man. It usually takes getting your heart stomped on a few times before you start to wise up and realize that you've been going about it all wrong.

The problem, y'see, is that while love may be all around us, it usually ends up hiding behind it's various cousins that look an awful lot like love… and it's incredibly easy to mistake them for the real thing. When your idea of relationships and romantic love is based on 80s New Wave albums and John Hughes movies, you end up with wildly unrealistic expectations, leading to a great deal of unhappiness for both you and your erstwhile romantic partner. It's one thing to think that love is supposed to be a Bonnie Tyler video full of over-the-top choruses and heartfelt power chords about how explosive and overwhelming love is, but it's another entirely to try to base an entire relationship around it.

Unfortunately, love is one of those things that you can't describe directly. At best you can talk around it, about how it feels and how it affects us, even the physical effects like the generation of oxytocin… which is great for poetry and sappy top-40 ballads, but really bad for trying to sort out how you feel when you don't have much of a basis for comparison.

If you are trying to base a relationship on what you assume is love but is really one of it's look-alike cousins, then you run the risk of needless heartbreak and disappointment when you realize that what you had was actually something much more fleeting.

...And It Feels Like Love

So before we get into love in and of itself, let's go over some of the things that we tend to confuse for love.

Puppy Love

Puppy love is usually our first brush with romantic love, especially as tween or teenager. Most often it's a school-boy or girl crush, frequently on someone out of one's league whether it be a popular peer or an adult. It's that adoring rush of affection that leaves us dumbstruck and twitterpated... and in some cases[6] leads us to basically follow the object of our affection around like a lost puppy looking for a belly rub. It's most noted by the tendency to inspire the sufferer to spend their time daydreaming about their crush and indulging in elaborate (if usually fairly chaste) fantasies about a relationship with them. It's an exciting rush of emotion that feels larger than life and is, in reality, about as shallow as a puddle and usually lasts about as long as tears in the rain.

For all that it's generally looked upon by people with a mix of bemused nostalgia and shame, puppy love (or first love) can actually be a powerful force and the after-effects can linger for a lifetime; almost everybody has fond memories of their first "love".

Lust

Imagine how it felt the first time you saw someone you were really into. Your heart starts to race. Your palms sweat but your mouth goes dry. Your throat seems like it's slammed shut, forcing you to swallow if you want to say anything beyond a low croak. You're actually so nervous that you're shaking. You find them almost undeniably desirable and you can't stop yourself from wondering what they're going to feel like when you're holding them against you as you kiss madly in a dark corner somewhere.

Sounds an awful lot like love at first sight, no?

What you're actually feeling are physical symptoms of arousal[7]. But if you're going to go by generations of pop culture, this is what you've been told that love feels like. And if you're relatively inexperienced — and honestly, sometimes if you *are* fairly experienced — it's easy to mistake sexual attraction for love... especially if you can't *act* on that attraction. After all, it's a quirk of the human psyche that we almost instinctively want what we can't have; a libidinous "grass is always greener", if you will. Wanting to bang out can make y o u   b l i n d   t o   s o m e b o d y ' s   fl a w s   a n d fundamental incompatibilities because your genitals can yell a lot louder than your brain.

Lust is an immediate physical reaction to someone, prompted by pheromones screaming "this person would make an excellent genetic partner for your offspring", not a quasi-psychic recognition that the two of you are actually soul-mates. It's about the propagation of your DNA, not hearts and flowers and cartoon birds. We have a lot of cultural hang-ups built into our concept of love, and one of them is that sexual desire and love are somehow one and the same.

They're not; they just happen to occur at the same time so frequently that we conflate the two. This leads to any number of problems, especially with the concept of monogamy. Our cultural definition of "love" contains the inherent idea that love means you don't want to have sex with other people. Unfortunately, our biology, which insists that we want to ensure the spread of our genetic line, tends to have very strong opinions of it's own and doesn't pay attention to things like social contracts. As a result, we end up with couples in crisis because they realize that one or the other or both are having pants-feelings for other people... oh noes, this means our love wasn't true!

Another common issue is that lust by itself makes for a poor basis for a long-term relationship. Lust and sexual attraction is all about immediacy; the need to reproduce as soon as possible as often as possible. It doesn't concern itself over emotional compatibility or desirable traits in a life-long partner, just in someone who would make a good genetic match. When lust has been sated... well, sometimes you realize that you can't actually stand the person you were just smashing genitals with, never mind looking forward to a years-long commitment.

Limerence

Limerence is also known as infatuation. Like it's younger brother, puppy-love, limerence tends to carry the sufferer away in a tidal wave of passion and excitement. It feels like an all-encompassing euphoria, leaving the sufferer feeling as though their head is stuffed with cotton candy and pure MDMA. He or she frequently seems to have lost several critical IQ points as they seemingly obsess about the object of their affection, from the way he runs his fingers through his hair to the way she adorable way she chews her food. Limerence makes people reckless, seemingly willing to make absurd, even stupid decisions in the name of their newfound "love". Their feelings are almost like an chemical high, causing them to feel like they're on top of the world and they can do anything because hey, they're in love man, and like, *nobody's* ever felt like this before.

It's an undeniable rush, one that makes you understand just what all those French poets and depressed Britpop singers were going on about. It leaves you feeling like the world is about to break out into a musical number and the universe itself is smiling at *you*, personally.

Unfortunately, the stratospheric highs tend to come with corresponding meteoric plunges into cthonian lows. Limerence burns like a grassfire: wild, out of control and over in a flash, leaving behind the charred ruins and the consequences of all the incredibly stupid shit you did when you were caught in the middle of it. As amazing as you felt with that initial rush, when limerence burns itself out — and it always does — you can be left completely devastated. Where before you were on top of the world, now you're left feeling as though everything you had was a lie and that your life as you know it is effectively over.

Much like lust, limerence often coincides and overlaps with love; in fact, a lot of limerence is what is frequently called "new relationship energy" or "the honeymoon period" when everything is beautiful and amazing and your lover can do absolutely no wrong. Limerence is passion mixed with sexual desire, brought on by hormones and oxytocin generation, helping to build a sense of trust and emotional bonding with one's partner. The problem, however, is that passion inevitably fades, no matter how strong it is at the start. In fact, the half-life of limerence and passion is somewhere between six months to a year on average. After that point, the immediate "stop what you're doing right the hell now" feeling for your partner starts to dwindle and fade to something less intense.

Many couples assume that this is a sign that something's wrong, that the ebbing passion and lack of rush from sheer physical contact with their partner means that their love is fading or worse, over. This is the cause of a great deal of unnecessary panic and turmoil for couples who don't realize that limerence is only the *starting* point of a relationship… and if they're not careful, it can be it's end point as well.

In fact, passion's wane is a natural and necessary part of deepening a relationship's emotional bonds… turning from infatuation into a deeper, more intimate emotion that we know as love.

What Is Love?

The problem with mistaking lust or limerence for love is that it's like mistaking the ignition for the car; it makes a lot of noise and catches your attention, but it's only a part of the whole. Love is a much more gradual emotion than we're taught to believe. That initial "love at first sight" or "falling head over heels" is a mix of lust and infatuation that helps bring people together. Love itself is a deepening of the emotional bond that may be started by sexual desire or an initial attraction; romantic love is more akin to an incredibly deep friendship than a constant state of cardiac arrhythmia and limbic overdrive. It's a feeling of emotional intimacy, rather than necessarily a physical attraction, a desire for partnership and unity rather than just the need for sexual release.

Love is actually much calmer than we're lead to believe; even when the passion fades and the lust ebbs, love leaves a contentment and compassion for one's partner. Love isn't about crazy emotional rushes and blind cherubs with missile weapons, it's about forging a long-term partnership with someone who you want by your side and at your back, offering compassion and support. Love is about finding a life-long partner in crime.

This isn't to say that love is blind or somehow makes someone oblivious to his or her partner's flaws, or that love is enough to overcome all obstacles. Quite the opposite, actually; more often than not, couples who are well and truly in love but are fundamentally incompatible frequently find that love simply isn't enough to make things work, no matter how much they wish it was.

However, love is the motivating force that makes them want to fight for their relationship and fix it rather than just let it fall apart.

How do you know when it's love?[8]

It's when you realize that no matter how annoyed or outright pissed you get at someone, that they're the one you want to spend all your time with. When you realize that they're someone you want guarding your back, helping you pick your ass up off the floor and sitting in the rocker next to you when the two of you are old and decrepit and wearing adult diapers... and you still think they're the coolest, sexiest motherfucker you know.

It's when, even when the passion is spent and the "new car smell" of the relationship has long faded that you can look over at them and realize.

Yup.

That's true love.

---

[1] There is no One. You don't have *one* soulmate out there. To quote Tim Minchin:

Your love is one in a million/

You couldn't buy it at any price/

But of the 9.999 hundred thousand other loves/

Statistically, some of them would be equally nice.

[2] And a host of other romantic comedies for good measure.

[3] From the French "chevalier", meaning "knight". Told you: blame the French.

[4] ...mostly.

[5] I'm really not joking here. Lancelot's inclusion into the Arthurian mythos is the equivalent of somebody's self-insert superhero joining the Avengers and banging Black Widow.

[6] i.e. me

[7] Or fear, for that matter. Your brain tends to decide which it is after the fact.

[8] Look, I've had this song stuck in my head the entire time I was writing this chapter. It's only fair that it's stuck in yours too.

PART TWO:
THE SECRETS OF A HAPPY RELATIONSHIP

You wouldn't think it, but one of the more nerve-wracking times in your relationship is when you realize it's starting to get serious. During your honeymoon period, everything feels natural and effortless. You don't fight and you find it impossible to believe that you *wouldn't* want to spend every waking hour with your partner.

But no matter how deliriously happy you may be, reality will inevitably reassert itself and you'll start to realize that your partner isn't the perfect being they were at the start. Those cute quirks they had before are starting to become annoying. You're beginning to find that you're appreciating those times when they're busy and you're left to your own devices. And of course, you've had your first fight. Possibly even your second, third or fourth.

This is the point when many couples start to freak out and worry that they've fallen out of love. In reality, however, they're discovering what *everyone* learns eventually: that relationships take work to maintain… and yours is no exception.

But work doesn't mean that those happy days are behind you. While the initial rush may fade, it's replaced by a deeper, more intimate connection with your partner. It takes nurturing and maintenance, but doing so also means that you're going to discover what it means to *be* someone's partner. That bond of trust and confidence means knowing that somebody has your back - in the brightest of days and the blackest of nights. They're your best friend, your compatriot, your partner in crime, your family by choice.

That's a relationship putting some effort into.

As with other forms of maintenance, the earlier you start, the fewer problems you have down the line, and the easier they are to fix. Nobody can guarantee that you won't have times of trouble, but learning these lessons now means that the happy days of your relationship will vastly outnumber the rough patches.

SEVEN

WHAT MAKES A RELATIONSHIP WORK?

The Secret To Making A Relationship Work is Putting In The Work

ONE OF THE trickiest parts of having a happy, successful relationship is, frankly, the relationship itself. Most of the time, when we try to work on improving our love-lives we focus on the early days and trying to find someone to date. It's easy to get tunnel vision in the early days, especially when you've been working so hard at the early stages — developing your approach, learning how to generate attraction, etc. — that once you start having some successes... you don't know quite what to do next. Like a dog chasing cars, we have no idea what we're supposed to do once we catch one. We've spent so much time focusing on trying to attract a lover in the first place that we never put any points into developing the skills to maintain the relationship we've been driving towards.

We're taught to have unrealistic expectations about relationships;

even when we understand intellectually that they take work and maintenance, in practice, we have a tendency to think that they're supposed to be exercises in self-perpetuating happiness. If we're lucky, we have our parents as role-models to pattern ourselves after. All too often, however, we're left to our own devices with only the vaguest notions of what a relationship is supposed to be.

It's easy as long as you're in the honeymoon stage, when your partner can do no wrong and her farts smell like angel smiles and rainbows, when even his bed-head is adorable and that weird noise he makes with his teeth when he's thinking is quirky, not annoying. But then reality sets in, like it always does, and we watch our relationships crash and burn without any idea what happened or how we could have prevented it.

Even under the best of circumstances, we usually learn these lessons through fucking up over and over again. And while some people do need to touch the stove before realizing that it's going to burn you, most of us would probably appreciate a warning or two before we end up making an unscheduled trip to the burn-ward.

When the New Relationship Smell starts to fade and those cute little quirks are starting to be the things that drive you crazy that determines whether or not you're going to have a long and happy relationship. If you want to have an amazing relationship, you have to know what it takes to make it last.

Remember the 5 to 1 Ratio

One of the oldest sexist clichés about women in relationships is that they will remember every single slight, mistake and argument, packing them away like a passive-aggressive squirrel burying hate-nuts for the winter... and pull them out at the worst possible moment during a fight.

Of course, it's not only women that do this; both men and women will bring up old grievances at the drop of a hat, keeping score in a perverse game of "who's less wrong" where the only winners are liquor stores and divorce lawyers. But there's actually a reason why those old conflicts hang around so prominently in our memory: the psychological phenomenon known as the negativity bias.

The negativity bias, simply put means we pay more attention and give more credence to the negative. Our brains react much more strongly to stimuli we perceive as negative, painful or unpleasant. The negativity bias is an evolutionary development that was meant to keep us alive when our biggest sources of stress was "not being eaten" instead of "Starbucks screwed up my latte". Being more aware of negative feelings gave us a sort of Spidey-sense that meant that we were better able detect and react to danger. Unfortunately, what was necessary to keep us alive back in the days when we lived in fear of saber-toothed cats, dire wolves and cave bears doesn't play well with our capacity for abstract reasoning. Negative thoughts weigh heavier on our minds than positive thoughts - and this includes the times our partners upset us. I'm not using a rhetorical flourish here; negative thoughts quite literally affect us five times more than positive ones. This ratio causes an interference effect – it's harder to appreciate the positives of something when there's a negative associated with it as well.

This is why all the ways our partner has upset us or "wronged" us stick with us far more easily than the happy times do — your brain pays more attention to those negative feelings and gives them a greater statistical weight. Whether it's that we don't seem to appreciate something nice they did for us or a moment of unthinking selfishness on our partner's part, those little moments of anger and pain linger far longer in our memories than the good times, and those add up. Since the bad moments have five times the impact that a positive one does, it takes approximately five good moments to each bad one to balance things out. If the ratio drops below 5 to 1 of positive to negative interactions, the relationship suffers.

Of course, it's almost impossible to keep track of every single accidental insult, snarky remark or hurt feeling, so attempting to keep an exact tally is absurd. Instead, you just want to make a point of doing *more* to make those happy moments happen. It doesn't need to be a constant stream of hearts and flowers — that's just as impossible to keep up indefinitely. But putting some conscious thought towards more deliberate acts of kindness, more moments of unprompted affection, more compliments and more thoughtful moments help negate the effect of the inevitable moments of conflict or inconsiderate words. Something as simple as making a point of telling your partner that you think they look good or that you appreciate them can make the difference between a long, happy relationship and a bitter break-up.

And speaking of positive moments...

Practice Gratitude

Want to make your relationship better? Spend time being grateful for your partner.

Scientists and psychologists have long documented that gratitude is intrinsically tied to happiness and well-being. People who practice gratitude and appreciation for others as well as their own blessings are consistently happier and healthier. It's not just a matter of passively feeling gratitude that gives that emotional boost; just as the the physical *act* of smiling makes you happier, actively practicing gratitude makes you more aware of just how lucky you are. This, in turn, improves your mood and outlook on life. It increases social ties between friends and family and makes you a more pleasant person. That, in turn, means that people feel happier and more relaxed in your presence. It helps you realize that even when things are bad, that you can always strive to make them better.

And while just being happier in general is a great reason to practice gratitude, spending time being appreciative for your partner and everything they bring to the table can improve your relationship as well.

When we're in relationships, we have a tendency to settle into certain roles and patterns of behavior. Even in the most egalitarian relationships, we tend to drift into roles that suit our skills and personalities — often without even thinking about it. One person will do a larger share of the housework for example, while the other may be the unofficial cook. The problem is that over the course of a long-term relationship, we tend to get used to the fact that our partners fill those roles... and if we're not careful, we even take them for granted. One of the surest ways to ruin a relationship is through indifference; no matter how much you may love cooking for your snugglebunny, if you feel like it's just something you're supposed to do, you're going to resent it.

Everyone wants to be reminded that someone we love thinks we're special and that they're glad we're part of their lives. It doesn't have to be something huge; nobody's asking for a standing ovation for doing the day to day chores and errands or making it through another day at a crappy job so you can pay your half of the rent. However, hearing that our partner notices the effort we put in to the relationship can have an immense effect on our mood and make it feel like it's worth it. It can turn something as basic as the daily tidying up from chore into an act of love. Taking the time to let your honey know — unprompted — that you appreciate the things they do lets them know that you're paying attention and that you're not taking their presence for granted.

More often than not, it's the little things that mean the most just because they're the things that we do that we think nobody notices. So take time — every day if you can — to remind your partner that you're grateful for them and for what they do for you. You'd be amazed at just how much happier your relationship will be when you do.

Have A Life Outside of Your Relationship

It's great that your honey-bunny is your best friend; that's actually one of the qualities that makes for a strong, lasting relationship. But that doesn't mean that he or she is your only friend. In fact, making them your sole source of support and companionship can put some serious stress on your relationship in the long run. One person can't be all things to all people, and it's a mistake to try. All too often couples — especially young ones — assume that they should do everything together and needing time apart is a sign that things are wrong. This is something that many couples struggle with. After all, one of the oldest relationship cliches is the man or woman who gets into a relationship and never sees their friends again.

In some relationships, they have to practically beg to get a night out with the guys or to spend more time with the girls. One enterprising company actually created an app that automatically texts a guy's girlfriend so you can have "more bro time". Nothing says "a relationship built to last" like having to beg to spend time with your friends, right guys?

(Ahem)

But it doesn't have to be that way. In fact, the happiest couples out there are the ones who have a vibrant and active social life *outside* of just the two of them. It's actually important for your emotional well-being – and your partner's – to maintain those relationships that aren't built exclusively on your being together. It helps maintain your identity as individuals outside of the state of your relationship and sustains your social networks that are vital to our emotional and physical health. It's especially important for men to maintain friendships outside of their relationship; straight men have a tendency to isolate themselves and rely on their partners as their sole source of emotional intimacy. This can put a significant burden on their girlfriends and wives and leave everybody feeling trapped and smothered. Having more people in your life to provide support and intimacy broadens your base and makes your entire relationship stronger.

It can be difficult for some couples to make time for people outside of their "couple" friends; some even see this as somehow sacrificing their own emotional intimacy for the sake of others. When you're in a relationship, it's only natural you're going to prioritize spending time with your partner over your friends, but that doesn't mean you shouldn't carve out time to spend with them — or even just some very necessary "me" time. In fact, I'll give you some tips on getting space within the relationship in later chapters.

Just remember: a designated game night with your buddies, planned outings, even just regular get-togethers to hang out and just catch up, can mean the difference between feeling trapped and a stronger, healthier relationship.

Have More Sex

OK, so this one is kind of a "duh George". After all, dissatisfaction with one's sex life — in all its many forms — is one of the most common reasons why couples break up, right after financial stresses. Hell, the idea that relationships are the death knell of sex is another of the oldest clichés that gets passed around. And to be fair: there's a certain level of truth to it. No matter how hot and heavy you and your partner may be at the beginning, the day to day stresses and responsibilities can make it hard to find the time or even throw your libidos out of whack so that one of you gets horny in the morning while the other's raring to go after the sun goes down.

And — let's be honest — once you've been together for a while, there will be plenty of times when one or both of you would rather pass on sex for a good night's sleep because hey, you've got that damn meeting in the morning and it's already 10:30 and… well…

Next thing you know, it'll have been weeks since the two of you have had any quality naked time together.

But this isn't just about keeping the spark in your relationship (more on that in part 3); it's about what sex does specifically to make your relationship maintenance easier.

See, sex is actually kind of goddamn amazing for your mental health and physical well-being. Having frequent sex helps alleviate stress and and depression, relieves physical pain, helps you sleep better and even improves your mood, making you calmer and more patient. Orgasms produce oxytocin — the chemical associated with feelings of love — which prompts emotional bonding, helping make you feel closer and more connected with your partner. Even physical affection without aiming for orgasms — cuddling, kissing, and so forth — helps encourage more emotional closeness and feeling more connected and in tune with one another.

The problem is that most of us just "let sex happen", instead of planning for it. When we leave having sex up to the moments when libidos and schedules align, we end up having less and less of it over time. That's why one of the unspoken secrets for having a happier relationship, is to schedule sex. Yeah, it doesn't seem like the most romantic thing in the world; in fact, at first, it can feel like you're turning sex from a form of intimacy within a relationship to "just another thing to check off the to-do list". In practice however, scheduling sex actually makes it *better*.

To start with: you're ensuring that you're carving out time in your day for sex instead of just hoping that you'll find the time for it. There are only so many hours in the day and everything in life — including sex — has an opportunity cost. If you don't specifically make time for sex, it becomes harder and harder to find the time to have it; other things just keep getting in the way.

But what about the times when you're just not *interested* in banging out at your scheduled time? Well, there're actually benefits to this as well. To start with: clearing out your schedule for squishy noises means you have time where other things aren't hanging over your head. You aren't as concerned about the other things that need to get done because you've been able to shift things around. Alleviating those stresses remove many of the issues that can kill your libido. Similarly, knowing that sex is going to happen actually builds anticipation. Knowing that sex is around the corner can make the rest of your week feel like a lead-up to the weekend... especially if you and your partner do a little playful flirting during the lead-up.

Even if you're not feeling horny when the appointed hour comes, it's good to stick to the schedule and start that make-out session as planned. Research shows that being "in the mood" often comes simultaneously with being physically aroused. So scheduling a make-out session and sticking to it even if you're not necessarily feeling horny may seem unromantic as hell... but you'll find that you're actually going to be ready to get down as you get into it and the blood starts flowing to your happy bits.

The tricky part is working out just how much sex is the *right* amount of sex. Despite what many relationship therapists have advocated for years, there is no "ideal" number of times to have sex per week or month. In fact, trying to hold yourselves to an arbitrary number can cause otherwise satisfied couples to feel as though they're doing something wrong if they go at it four times one week and zero the next. This is why it's important to actually talk about your sex lives — what your expectations are, what you'd like more of, what you'd like less of and negotiating a compromise of how often you'd like to be having it that satisfies you both. Not only does negotiating your intimacy mean that both of you will be more satisfied — after all, good negotiation means that both sides are getting their needs met — but studies have shown that couples who hash out their sex lives together wind up feeling closer and more intimate.

Sounds like a win-win to me.

Expect More (and Be More)

The worst part about settling down means... well, *settling*.

Not for your partner, but for settling into a routine, day to day existence. Humans are prone to what's known as hedonic adaptation; we can get used to literally *anything*. Everything in our lives becomes the day to day, including being in a relationship with someone amazing, someone who's so amazing that we can't believe they're dating us. Eventually, that honeymoon period when we want to impress them and try to show them nothing but our best, most attractive selves comes to an end and... well, some things just don't seem as important as they once did.

We get comfortable enough with them — and with our relationship — that we're not worried about them seeing us when we've woken up hung over as hell and feeling like someone puked in our brain and the fact that we've bothered putting on pants should be considered an amazing accomplishment. When you can feel your hair growing, it's hard to care about little things like deodorant or foundation.

We're not as worried about being perfect. We're ok with them seeing us in our "don't give a fuck" sweats. We allow ourselves to be a bit less conscientious, a little more self-absorbed. We begin to take them — and their feelings for us — for granted. We, quite frankly, let ourselves get a little lazy. So we don't put in as much effort. We don't worry about being as entertaining for our partners. We dial back our personal maintenance routines and dress a little more for comfort than for looks on our downtime. We let ourselves order the double-cheese pizza with extra cholesterol when we normally would've gotten the pasta primavera, spend a little less time on the personal grooming and just begin to settle in. We fall into ruts. Routines. Go on automatic.

And because we take our cues from our nearest and dearest... our partners tend to do so as well. And this can be a mistake.

Don't get me wrong: I'm not saying that everyone has to be on their best behavior at all times or that you can't relax into a relationship, especially a long-term one. Being comfortable with your partner is one of the best parts of a relationship; you're finally in a place where you can let it all hang out, figuratively and literally. And after all, time and gravity are going to have their way with us all in the end.

But the couples who last are the ones who expect more from their partners... and from themselves. Part of what makes them last is that they still make a point of acting like they're just starting out together. These are the couples who continue to put in effort to keep things going — making a point of showing interest in what their partners have to say or to share new experiences with them, celebrating triumphs, even taking care of themselves.

It doesn't have to be a huge production. You don't need to be constantly proving your love by hiring sky-writers to cover the sky with love poems to your sweetie or taking them on candle-lit gondola tours of Venice[1]. You just have to be willing to put in a little more effort. Make a point to take care of yourself so you're still sexy for your partner, whether this is hitting the gym or putting more care into the way you dress and put yourself together. Give a little more affection. Take some time to just be together without distractions. Treat date night like it's your *first* date instead of "our usual Friday night," and take your partner to the places you'd go when you want to impress somebody. Just a little more effort at putting your best self forward will make your partner feel amazing… and they'll want to put more effort in to please you as well.

Don't Forget That You're In This Together

Something I see fairly often in nerd couples — my core readership — is the tendency to compartmentalize their individual lives from their life together. In some ways it can seem perfectly logical: this event/series of circumstances/disaster happened to me specifically, therefore it shouldn't affect/upset you. Except… it totally does. Even if you're not living together, you're still part of "Team Us"; what affects one of you is going to materially affect both of you, even if it's not immediately obvious.

Sometimes it's a minor thing; bad shit is happening at work/ with your friends/ your World of Warcraft guild, which means you're not going to be able to hang out with your sweetie as often. Sometimes it's major; you've just discovered you've got some horrible disease, you've been laid off from work, a family member is having a major crisis. Either way, these are going to affect your partner as well as you because, well, you're *partners*. It's right there in the name. Part of the whole *point* of relationships is that you're sharing your lives together; what affects one of you is going to materially affect the both of you, even if it just means that your snugglebunny is having to double up on being your cheerleader and a source of strength.

That's the thing about relationships. If you're at all serious, then it means that the two of you are going to have to face the good times and the bad times together. You can't segregate some aspect off and pretend that it doesn't affect your partner too.

You don't just want someone who's there with you for some of the good times... you want someone who's there for all of them and who's got your back when things go bad.

Because in the end, it always comes down to the two of you, and if you want a partner in crime, you want someone who's going to be there with you to back you up when it's time to tell the Universe that you're going to throw down.

---

[1] ...though it certainly won't *hurt*.

EIGHT
HOW TO FIGHT... THE RIGHT WAY

This Isn't 'Nam, Donnie, There're Rules.

ONE OF THE most dangerous times in a relationship are the days following the Honeymoon Period.

See, during the Honeymoon Period, everything is amazing. The world beams at you with beneficence. . Every morning cartoon birds fly in through your window to make you breakfast while fat happy mice serenade the two of you. Life is a grand adventure with you and your partner who is such a Perfect Being that he or she farts rainbows and cotton candy.

She doesn't have flaws, she has idiosyncrasies. His snoring and propensity to get distracted by whatever shiny object flits within his field of vision isn't annoying, it's adorable. And every single person in this stage of the relationship will inevitably say those same three words:

"We never fight."

You might as well say "I'll be right back" or "What else could go wrong?", for as we all know, the strongest force in the Universe is irony and saying "We never fight" is the karmic equivalent of climbing a mountain top and shouting "GOD HAS SHITTY AIM!" at the top of your lungs.

Which means, of course, that The Fight, with capital letters is going to happen. And that fight could very well be the *last* one you have.

Like I said before: relationships are kind of like *Fight Club*: if you're you're dating someone, you're going to fight. There's no getting around it. It's the inevitable result of being in a relationship with another person: there's going to be conflict, no matter how drift compatible you may be.

The sooner you accept this, the sooner you can learn how to *stop* fighting.

Rather than trying to avoid conflict, people in the most successful relationships learn *how* to fight so that they don't end up doing more damage to one another. But learning how to fight is only part of the answer. You also have to know how to *stop* fighting so that you can actually fix things and move on to the more important parts of the relationship... like the make-up sex.

If you don't know how to argue properly, you do risk doing damage to the relationship... or worse, being cut off from sex for who knows how long.

If you're going to fight, you have to know how to argue correctly. You need to follow the rules.[1]

Rule #1: Keep Your Cool

I know you're angry. You may have a perfectly legitimate reason to be angry. You're so incredibly pissed that clouds of cartoon steam are pouring out your ears and that vein in your temple is pounding like a Rick Allen drum solo. You can hear the volume in your voice rising the longer that the argument goes on…

Well, clamp it down, soldier. You need to keep your head straight while you're arguing and yelling isn't going to help matters. In fact, it's just going to make things worse.

When you're arguing with your partner, your anger — however justified it may well be — can only work against you. When you get angry, you don't think straight. You don't pay *nearly* as much attention to what you're saying… or what your partner is saying, for that matter. You'll interpret things in ways that they never intended, you'll assume the worst and you'll be far, far more tempted to get your digs in instead of trying to resolve the argument.

Think of it this way. Arguments are like low-burning fires. Approach it in the right way and it'll go out with minimal fuss. Yelling and losing your temper, on the other hand, is like tossing a bottle of lighter fluid into the mix. Sometimes the explosion will consume the fuel quicker and end things. Most of the time though, it's going to start burning out of control and in ways you didn't account for. And you're probably going to lose your eyebrows in the process.

Don't get me wrong: I'm not saying that anger is *bad*. In fact, when properly harnessed, anger is an incredibly useful and important tool. However, anger is rarely a rational emotion. It's almost impossible to have a practical discussion with your partner when you're caught up in anger; it's entirely too easy to get distracted by side issues or to dredge up old issues to justify why you're so pissed right now. And like

like that fire, anger can be deceptive. Just because the immediate argument is over doesn't mean that you're not still ticked off. It may seem like things are settled, but one errant spark and suddenly the whole thing flares up again and burns the forest down.

If you want to stop fighting and actually fix things, then you need to give yourself time to cool down. Separately.

Yes, separately. It can be hard to let go of things when the person who's ticking you off is right there with you; you end up feeling pressured to say you're OK, even if you're still angry. So the best thing you can do is get a little bit of space and let yourself calm down.

You want to get away from the scene of the argument (which is going to just keep reminding you of the fact that you've had one) and do the things that let you cool off. Take a walk. Hit the gym and jump on the treadmill and burn out that fire by exhausting yourself. Go listen to music that helps calm you down.

What you *shouldn't* do is do the things that you may *think* you should do. Don't punch that pillow — or that heavy bag, for that matter. *Don't* go into a room and yell incoherently. *Don't* play any deathmatches online or assume that some uber-violent video game is going to let you vent your anger. Aggressive behavior — even when you're by yourself — just *reinforces* your anger. It stokes it and keeps the flames going. Instead, you want to do the things that calm you down and cool you off instead.

There are a lot of people who will tell you that you *shouldn't* walk off, that every argument should be resolved right then and there. This is a spectacularly, crossing-the-streams-level bad idea; not every conflict is one that *can* be resolved in one sitting and trying to do so while you're still angry makes it next to impossible. It's better to take time to vent, decompress and come back when you're cool and collected.

Just make sure you let your partner know what you're doing and why; just standing up and storming out is a great way to really hurt someone. Tell them: "Look right now I'm too angry to think straight. I need to go do X to calm down so we can sort this out. I'll be back in 15 minutes/a half hour/an hour."

I know this part is difficult, especially when you're 100% correct or you feel as though you're being treated unfairly. Trust me: take a deep breath, hold it, let it out slowly. Let your heart rate slow a little before you speak. Tell your partner that you need to cool off for a moment, exit the scene, take a few minutes to calm the fuck down before you get back in there and continue in a reasonable manner. It's easier to fight properly when you can keep your wits about you.

If you can't... well, I hope your couch is comfy.

Rule #2: Ask Yourself "Is This The Hill You're Willing To Die On?"

Here's something that trips a lot of people up: sometimes we pick the wrong battles, whether we're the aggressor or not. We get upset over the wrong things. We get into fights – or make fights worse – because we don't stop to ask ourselves whether the fight is one worth having.

One of the most common conflicts in relationships involves the desire to be "correct" rather than "right". Chalk it up to how men and women are socialized; men are taught that they're supposed to be "doers" while women are the "feelers". Men tend to look for concrete "do this and things will be better" solutions to conflicts. Unfortunately, one of the ways that we tend to express this is by pointing out that the other person is mistaken or doesn't understand.

This works about as well as using nitro glycerine to clean the stove.

Let me tell you: there's nothing like telling a person "no, you're wrong" to turn a minor fight into a major confrontation. This is a really bad idea when your goal is to stop fighting in the first place.

If we take the classic domestic conflict of "you don't help me do the dishes" and respond with all the ways that we *do* contribute (paying the bills, picking up around the house, whatever) then we're trying show that what we do is an equivalent exchange... which it may well be in terms of comparative time/effort spent, but that doesn't actually address the issue.

The issue isn't that you're not doing your share, it's that you're making your partner feel unappreciated. By going into detail about why they're wrong, all that you're doing is telling them that *they don't have the right to feel the way they feel*. Now not only are you ignoring the underlying issue, but you've told them that they are wrong for having needs in the first place.

Similarly, yeah, your girlfriend may have seen what *looked* like you flirting with the cute redhead from Accounts Receivable, but clearly nothing was going on, therefore it's completely unreasonable for her to be mad at you! Congratulations, you've fallen victim to one of the classic blunders, the most famous of which is "You're being completely irrational," but only slightly less well known is this: nobody ever believes you when you say "This isn't what it looks like!" You may not be in the wrong, but saying "You're not allowed to feel this way because I am correct in this matter" doesn't actually change how your behavior made them feel.

Being factually correct doesn't mean that you're actually in the right – especially when it's not about the "facts" but about how a person's behavior makes the other person feel. Being "correct" isn't going to win you any points, especially when your partner's seeing it from a completely different perspective. "Winning" the argument is a pyrrhic victory when it ruins the relationship in the process, especially when it's over comparatively minor details.

The problem with this approach is that we tend to equate being correct with having the moral high-ground that immediately puts *everybody* on the defensive. Suddenly you're feeling unfairly attacked while they're is hearing you tell them that they are wrong for feeling hurt in the first place. Now you're both put in the position where you're no longer actually addressing the problem, you're arguing about who's "right" and there's no real way to back down without losing face. Now you're fighting to defend your ego and there's no real way to "win" without losing at the same time.

This doesn't mean you have to back down every time, nor does it mean that you're honor-bound to sit there and not defend yourself. You can — and *should*— give your side of things, especially if you feel that something was mistaken. However, *don't* frame it as who's right and who's wrong. Instead, you want to focus on what you were thinking, how *you* saw your actions. It's "OK, I see where you're coming from, here's where *I* was coming from," not "you aren't factually right, therefore you can't be mad at me".

You have to ask yourself: "Is this really the hill I want to die on?" Are you really willing to prolong the fight, or even make it worse, rather than just swallowing your pride and listening to what she's actually saying? How much is being "right" worth to you, especially when it comes at the expense of how your partner feels?

Rule #3: Don't Aim To Wound

The next rule when it comes to fighting is simple: don't say the things you *know* are going to hurt your partner. Intimacy can be a double-edged sword; when you and your partner have lowered your defenses and let one another in, it means you've also deliberately made yourselves vulnerable to one another. On the one hand, this promotes a level of closeness and emotional bonding that strengthens your relationship to one another and lets you understand each other on a more primal level. At the same time, it means you know *all* of their insecurities, neurosis and deep dark fears... and that means that you know *exactly* where to stick the knife to inflict the most amount of pain.

And during a fight, there's a temptation to do just that. It's an ugly part of our psyche that we all try to keep in check. But there are times when it's all too easy for that part of us to slip the leash.

When your blood is pumping and your temper is high and you're full of righteous indignation because you feel that you're being unfairly maligned, it can be incredibly tempting to lash out. You're hurt and you want to strike back any way you can. The problem, of course is this doesn't get you any closer to actually resolving the issue. In fact, it makes things *worse*. Name calling, insults, preying on insecurities, pulling out old grievances... all of these become weapons in a war of escalation between two parties who know each other's weak spots and can aim a critical hit for maximum damage.

Not only is it childish and counter-productive, this sort of fighting can cause a mortal wound to your relationship. The worse the fighting and name-calling, the greater likelihood that one of you is going to say something that you can't take back. The wrong thing said in anger can bring even the strongest relationship to a grinding halt.

So how do you make sure you're not aiming to wound? Start with your body language. As weird as it may seem, our *bodies* influence our mood… not to mention how others respond to us. That clenched jaw, narrowed eyes and crossed arms are all universal signs of anger and defensiveness; the longer we feel the physical sensations, the more they make our *brains* feel angry and defensive. The angrier that you get… well, the more likely you are to say something hurtful. Being aware of your body gives you the opportunity to uncurl and unclench. Take a deep breath, unfold your arms and let your muscles relax, *especially* the muscles around your face. The sense of everything loosening up will hit you with a profound sense of relief and help drain much of your anger.

This, incidentally, will *also* help with your argument in general; by opening up your body language and adopting a less angry posture, you're going to be telling your partner that you're making a point of trying to calm down and *listen* to them.

Another important factor in not fighting to wound: slow your roll. That deep breath I told you to take will *also* force you to pause and *not* say what was just on the tip of your tongue. Taking that moment before you say anything keeps you from impulsively throwing whatever insult or rejoinder you had at the ready, and gives the signal that you're considering what your partner said before immediately launching into your own defense.

That delay can save your relationship. If you're, say, arguing about who hit the data cap on your ISP and your ego demands that you get your own back and you let fly with that *one* barb you know is going to wedge in their soul… well, suddenly you're not fighting about the bills any more. Now you're desperately trying to fix the emotional equivalent of an iron prybar through the mid-section.

Your relationship may survive… but it's gonna have one hell of a scar afterwards.

Rule #4: Stick To the (Real) Issue At Hand

Speaking of arguing the right way, the next important rule is very simple: one fight at a time. When couples fight, there's an almost inevitable impulse to turn this *one* fight into a referendum on *everything* that's wrong in the relationship and derailing the entire argument. You start off arguing about who left the seat up again, which turns into who made the two of you so late for the party last week which somehow further mutates into a fight about who is contributing what to the household and that iPad you shelled out for.

Now you've turned what was a simple disagreement to an Airing of Grievances as the two of you dig up all those hidden stores of grudges and slights that you've been storing in your emotional go-bag like a Relationship Apocalypse Prepper. The deeper you dip into that well of unresolved affronts, the more likely you're going to pull out one of the Forbidden Insults and end up breaking Rule #3.

Letting yourself get derailed by bringing up *other* topics, no matter how much you feel they're relevant to the issue at hand, means that you're never going to make any progress towards resolving what made you blow up at each other in the first place. Some arguments can be so protean and malleable that before too long you don't even remember what the hell set things off, just that the two of you are pissed off at each other for something which is almost certainly their fault. Meanwhile, the real problem – she feels that she has to fight to get your attention while you have all the time in the world for your buddies; you're feeling as though you're not allowed to have time to yourself, while she runs your life with clockwork precision – continues to fester just below the surface.

Keep diversions to a minimum, without rehashing old fights or side-issues, by focusing on the end-result. What is the fight about? What needs to be resolved? Stick to that goal. Getting distracted by other matters only delays actually resolving whatever matter started the fight in the first place.

A side note: if you find that the topic of the fight keeps changing, this is a good sign that the real problem isn't what you're arguing about. Go back to rule #2 and start listening to what your partner is really saying.

Rule #5: The Fighting Needs To Stop Before You Can Fix Things

The key to resolving a conflict in your relationship isn't to avoid fighting or argue more effectively... it's to *stop* fighting in the first place. As long as the two of you are debating the existence of the problem in the first place — whether it's getting your partner to recognize the problem *is* a problem or the two of you are engaging in a battle of "less-wrong-er-than-thou" — then you're not actually fixing things. You're just throwing verbal flack at one another.

Fixing things can't happen until the fighting stops. Ideally, this will happen you've both calmed down and gotten to a point where you're able to talk about things like reasonable people, even you haven't quite managed to forgive each other yet. Other times, it comes down one one of you to be willing to back down. This can be incredibly difficult, especially once egos are on the line and you don't want to admit that maybe you're wrong. Just remember rule #2: sometimes you need to recognize that some fights aren't worth "winning".

This doesn't mean that you should try to quash the fight immediately. Sometimes fights need to happen for people to even realize there's a problem in the first place. But this *does* mean that the two of you should put a priority on calming down and remembering the love at the core of your relationship.

This is the time to work out a resolution to the cause of the fight. It's great that you've stopped fighting but that's just treating a symptom. Unless you actually address the cause, then all you've done is just put things on pause until you fight again.

Resolving the conflict should be a collaborative approach. This means you have to work together to fix things, not just dictate terms to one another as though you're negotiating the Treaty of Versailles. You want to ask two questions:

First: "What do you need to make things better?"

Then: "How can we make this happen?"

Please notice that order of pronoun usage, because that "we" is important, no matter who was "in the wrong" in a fight. Relationships are inherently a partnership; you're supposed to be working *together* towards a common goal and understanding. They're not about "who wins" and "who loses"; *everyone* loses when you're fighting, no matter who's actually in the right. Collaborating together to find a way to make things right reinforces the fact that at the end of the day, *you're on the same side.*

It's worth noting: not every solution is going to be a compromise. Sometimes you have to be willing to accept that what you've done has hurt your partner and that you're going to need to make concessions in the name of not hurting them or vice versa. That's part of the price of entry to being in a relationship with someone; if you're unwilling to pay it… well, then you probably shouldn't be in a relationship with them in the first place.

Rule #6: Apologize. The Right Way

The fastest way to stop fighting is simple: apologize. But you can't just say "well, sorry" and expect everything to be magically ok. You have to apologize the *right* way.

This is another area that trips a lot of people up: we tend to equate apologizing with being morally wrong. Why should we apologize when we don't believe we've done anything wrong?

Well... because like I said earlier: being "correct" doesn't mean that you're "right". Apologizing isn't just about who's wrong or who's right. It's also about taking responsibility for how you've made someone feel. A sincere apology means understanding *why* your partner is upset with you and copping to your part in having made it happen.

First: make sure you understand what you're actually apologizing *for*. After all, apologizing for the wrong thing is going to sound like you're being snarky and insincere and risk pissing them off *again*... even if you don't mean to. The best way to do make sure you get what you're apologizing for is simple: try to summarize your understanding as to why they're upset. "You're upset because you saw me flirting with Helena, am I right?" for example. Then listen. Don't defend yourself – just listen to why they're upset. Then apologize for it. "I understand. I'm sorry I hurt you by doing X."

Did you do something wrong? That's (sometimes) debatable. What *isn't* debatable is the way you made them feel. And if you actually care about the person you're dating, then you damn well better care about not hurting them.

Notice very carefully that this is the active voice. There is nothing more infuriating than a weaselly non-apology apology like "I'm sorry you were hurt"; it's a verbal way of putting the blame on *them* for being unreasonable, rather than taking responsibility for your part in hurting them. Similarly, you never give an apology with a qualifier. Saying "I'm sorry, but..." is telling somebody that not only are you *not* sorry but once again, they're wrong for feeling that way in the first place.

(To pre-empt the obvious objection: if you feel that your partner is consistently unreasonable about the way they feels, then it's probably well past time the two of you broke up. Either you're right and they're impossible, in which case you shouldn't be dating them in the first place or they're right and you're the asshole and *they* shouldn't be dating *you*. Same result either way.)

And above all else: never, ever apologize *just* to make the fight stop and get someone off your back. This not only invalidates the apology – because you're *not* sorry – but tells people that you're not going to do anything about it. You're essentially interacting on bad faith- you have no intentions of actually resolving the problem, you just want them to shut up. This is incredibly insulting on just about every level and is only going to hasten the inevitable demise of your relationship.

Also important: if you're the one being apologized to, accept the apology without editorializing. Responding to "I'm sorry, I was an asshole" with "Yup, you were" is just going to start the fight all over again.

Rule #7: Take Time To Make Up

You've managed to stop fighting. You've worked together to find a solution. Now it's time to make up... and in many ways, this is the most important part of arguing with your partner. You may have patched up the issues from the fight, but you're both still going to feel the sting of the fight and those lingering emotions can poison your relationship if you don't take care of them.

Now I know I said that most people get the wrong idea from "Don't go to bed angry." This doesn't mean that you need to quash the fight, it's that you need to resolve the pain that the fight *caused*. Going to sleep can actually preserve negative emotions or even make them worse. It doesn't do you any good to try to stop fighting if all you're going to do is cement the anger and hurt.

This is why making up is important. You're not *just* resolving the problem, you're reminding one another that even though you may fight, you still have that core of love and affection for one another. Yes, you may get angry, but that doesn't mean that at the end of the day, you don't love each other. It's important to keep that in sight.

Taking the time to make up afterwards is a form of relationship self-care. It's a way of reinforcing the bond and making each other happy again. You're soothing the hurt that you've both caused and replacing it with love and contentment. It reaffirms the strength of your relationship and rewards you for fixing the problems instead of just fighting over and over again.

And besides… if you don't take time to make up, when are you going to have that awesome make-up sex when you *do* stop fighting?

---

[1] Yes, yes, we've *all* seen that Monty Python sketch Mr. Clever Boots.

NINE
DRAMA-PROOF YOUR RELATIONSHIP

Don't Start None, Won't Be None

WE TALK A lot about "drama" when it comes to relationships and how to avoid it. Drama — in this case, unnecessary or manufactured conflict — is frequently the boogieman of dating; go to any online dating site and you'll see hordes of people declaring that they're a "drama-free zone" or have "no time for drama". We all realize how much drama can sabotage an otherwise healthy relationship and why it's so important to establish and maintain healthy boundaries in order to drama-proof our lives.

But we rarely ever stop to think that *we* might be the ones causing drama.

It's an easy thing to overlook. We tend to see drama as being something other people do. Men especially tend to see themselves as drama-free zones; even among otherwise egalitarian and feminist men, there's a tendency to equate "drama" with women. But drama is gender agnostic. Drama isn't restricted to any particular sexuality. Men of all stripes are just as prone to creating unnecessary conflict as women… we just don't get called on it as often. There's a saying I'm fond of: if you encounter an asshole one day, you've met one asshole. If you're constantly surrounded by assholes you're probably the asshole. Similarly, if every person you've ever dated is a drama-bomb… well, let's remember who's the sole common denominator in those relationships.

When it comes to relationships, we're responsible for our *own* behavior, not controlling our partner's. Making sure your relationship is a drama-free zone is more than just making sure that you're dating emotionally mature partners; it also means not creating that drama yourself.

Check Yourself

One of the biggest lies we tend to tell ourselves is that we're perfectly rational and objective when it comes to our own lives. It takes a lot of emotional energy to be completely honest with ourselves or to assess ourselves objectively. We have a massive host of cognitive biases that color how we see the world and how we see ourselves, and it's incredibly easy to justify ourselves to paint us in the most positive light. As a result: it's pretty easy to end up blind to some of your own flaws or mistakes.

Sometimes you have to look at things from a different angle to get much needed perspective. So with that in mind, I want you to answer some questions as honestly as you can.

- Do you often feel like your partner or your friends just don't understand you?

- Do your friends, family or partner describe you as "high-maintenance"?

- Are you easily irritated by things that other people seem to brush off as minor or unimportant?

- Do you argue with your family or loved ones often, especially about minor issues?

- Do you seem to find yourself surrounded by people who are jealous of you or who want to sabotage you?

- Are you continually frustrated people don't get it when they're just wrong?

- Do your friends, family or partner seem to refuse to see things the way you do, leading to fights?

  - Do those fights never seem to end? Do they drag out for hours or flare up repeatedly?

- Do your friends, family or partner accuse you of needing to be the center of attention?

- Do you seem to move from crisis to crisis, where everything seems to constantly go wrong?

  - When it does, is it usually someone else's fault?

- Does your partner never seem to listen to your side of things, but accuses you of not listening?

- Are you frustrated because people never seem to see why things aren't your fault?

- Do you feel that your partner takes other people's sides against you too frequently?

- Do you feel like your partner never gives you the credit or acknowledgement you deserve?

Individually, these questions don't mean anything in and of themselves. After all, sometimes our friends or partners really *don't* get it. Sometimes when things go tits-up it legitimately *is* someone else's fault. That being said, however, the more of these questions you answer "yes" to, the greater the possibility that *you* could be the source of much of the conflict in your relationship.

Now don't get me wrong. I'm not saying you're an asshole or a bad person. Most of the time, we're completely unaware that we're acting this way — we're too stuck in our own heads and don't see how the way we're behaving or responding is affecting the people that we care about. It can be hard enough to admit that there's even a problem, never mind that we're the cause. But this behavior ruins relationships and makes it hard to improve or even *form* meaningful, long-term relationships with friends, family or romantic partners.

So if these questions have you worried that you're causing unnecessary drama in your relationships, let's look at the things you can do to help prevent it.

Unnecessary relationship drama tends to come down to specific issues: a need for control, an inability to communicate clearly, a need for validation or a lack of self-awareness. Here's how to fix them.

Defusing The Drama Bomb By Using Your Words

One of the things that causes unnecessary conflict in relationships is simply not being understood. One of the oldest, hoariest tropes in fiction — especially when romance is involved — is how poor communication causes problems that could easily have been avoided. But as much as we may shake our heads at Ross and Rachel[1] for not fixing things with a simple conversation, we rarely recognize how often miscommunication complicates our own relationships. If you're continually complaining that your family, friends or partners never understand you... well, it may be that you're not making yourself clear.

One of the biggest ticking drama bombs in relationships is the tendency to assume that your partner is a mind-reader. Most arguments — especially in long-term relationships — tend to have two levels: what the fight is about on the surface and what's *really* wrong. The problem arises when we expect our partners to divine what we *really* mean without actually saying the words. Unfortunately, unless you're dating Jean Grey or the Martian Manhunter, you're not dealing with a telepath, you're dealing with an ordinary person and those surface details are going to complicate the issue. It's the classic "I want you to *want* to do the dishes" scenario — when someone says this, what they really mean is they want consideration and appreciation from their partner, not someone with a cleaning fetish. But that surface issue — the dishes — becomes a distraction and the meaning is lost.

To help communicate your point clearly, especially when there's a conflict, you want to focus on the *goal*, not the details. The details can be argued, nitpicked and otherwise derail the discussion — what do you mean by X, why do you say Y when I did Z, etc. When you're having an argument, ask yourself: what change are you hoping for? If things went exactly as you wanted, what would happen? Why would this be better than the situation as things are now? Those answers help you drill down to what you really want. Keeping that goal clear during the discussion helps keep things straight-forward.

Sometimes the problem isn't that you're getting distracted; the problem is that you're arguing about two entirely different things or that you have different ideas about what you're asking for. Making sure you're on the same page is an important step towards resolving conflicts. If your partner thinks you're asking for something absurd or insane, they're going to assume that you're being unreasonable; they may assume that you're picking a fight for drama's sake rather than trying to address sincere, heartfelt issues. The ur-example is, of course, from *Friends*: whether Ross and Rachel were on a break or not. Rachel having an idiosyncratic definition of what "being on a break" meant ultimately engendered the ongoing fight between the two of them. When you feel like you're not being understood, stop and ask your partner to explain what they think you're asking for... and listen. Don't get angry at them for not intuiting your real meaning or attack them for misunderstanding you, clarify things, preferably in simple terms. If you need something that you feel is lacking, then *use your words* and *ask for it specifically*.

It's worth remembering that clarity is critical when it comes to resolving miscommunication issues rather than speed. Many people need a moment or two to figure out how to phrase things properly; when they speak off the cuff they may misspeak, use the wrong words or generally create misunderstandings. If you have a tendency to say the wrong thing or aren't sure exactly how to phrase things, take your time. Don't let your partner prod you into a response; get actual distance if need be so you can organize your thoughts. Tell them "I need a few minutes to figure out how to say this. I'm going to go to the other room/ take a walk/ get some quiet until I can make sure I know what I'm trying to say." That time to choose your words can make the difference between fixing the problem or letting another misunderstanding turn a disagreement into full-blown drama.

Ask Yourself: Why Do You Need To Be Right?

You're a good person. You *know* you're a good person. That's why it's not your fault when things go wrong. You knew what to do, and if people would just listen to you, everything would be fine. But no, you put yourself out there and nobody seems to acknowledge it or shows any gratitude. They're the ones who're screwing you over...

So why doesn't *anyone* see this?

One of the most insidious causes of unnecessary drama is the need to control the narrative — to be "right" and, more importantly to have other people *agree* that you're right. It's a way of finding and maintaining power — especially when you may feel powerless otherwise. By being "right" and demanding that others conform to your world-view, you're insisting that others validate your beliefs — in essence, expressing power over them. It may be that you want them to acknowledge that you're uniquely disadvantaged by the universe, that you have barriers and limitations that are out of your control and that things are not your fault. It may be getting them confirm that other people are wronging you, confirmation that you're a righteous person who's maligned by others. It may manifest in arguing details rather than core problems in order to delegitimize someone else's anger or complaints; you're wrong about X, Y and Z, therefore you have no right to be angry at me. By continuing to do so, you are persecuting me.

You are, in essence, fighting for the right to define reality in your favor.

That need to be right, to constantly have one's world-view validated, is incredibly toxic; it makes relating to others increasingly impossible because disagreements become attacks. People who disagree with you are challenging your prerogative to claim the moral high-ground and the righteousness of your cause. It makes every interaction a struggle for frame control and social power because giving up that illusion of power means ceding a worldview that demands that others serve your needs without your having to admit or take ownership those needs. Not being "right" means that you may have to acknowledge your failures and deal with the consequences of your actions. It justifies your lack of power in a given situation by making you a victim... regardless of your own involvement in the matter.

If you're continually finding yourself fighting over whether or not people have a right to be upset with you or when people continually "refuse" to see or experience the world the exact same way you do, it's time to ask yourself just why it's so important that they agree with you. Will their conceding to your view change anything... or will it be a reason why you shouldn't have to change?

Take Control By Taking Responsibility

One of the ways we cause drama in relationships is by looking to deflect responsibility. The perpetual victim — the person who lurches from crisis to crisis when everything is going wrong and they need rescue — is seeing approval and affection... but doesn't want to take ownership of those needs. Similarly, the person who insists that they're being victimized by others, whether it's women, society, or just the universe itself, is seeking ways of absolving themselves from failure. The refuge in victimhood creates a narrative around being prevented from succeeding either through the machinations of others or just the sheer unfairness of the universe. If things were fair, then they'd totally succeed but since they aren't...

The logic of the surrender of personal autonomy gets especially twisted into salty tear-soaked pretzel shapes when the victimizer (such as the varying flavors of Straw Feminists imagined by various Men's Rights Activist groups) are simultaneously able to persecute the individual while *also* being inherently inferior. It allows the "victim" both the indignity of being robbed while also being superior in every way to their persecutors.

This particular form of drama is especially irritating to their friends because of their staunch refusal to do anything about it. Offers of help or suggestions on how to improve things are inevitably met with a "yes but…" or reasons why it couldn't possibly work, regardless of whether or not they'd tried it before.

That abdication of responsibility is a response to feeling powerless to affect meaningful change. But the secret to untying this particular drama-inducing knot isn't to give up control, it's to take it *back*. You may not be able to control others' actions or behavior – whether women refuse to date you, your co-workers act like dicks and shirk their responsibilities without consequence, etc. – but you can control your own. If you're convinced that your partner doesn't listen or understand, you focus on being clearer, finding ways to present yourself more effectively and communicating more productively — things that are within your control. If your co-workers fuck off — something *out* of your control — you focus on your *own* productivity and refuse to take responsibility for *their* work. If you fail to succeed at something, *own* your failure so that you can do better next time. When people offer you assistance, take it… with the knowledge that you have to do the work in order to solve your problem.

People only have so much sympathy for a victim. It's one thing to be a casualty of fate; it's another to be a perpetual loser who refuses to lift a finger to help themselves.

Eliminate Drama By Learning To Accept Yourself

One of the hardest parts of avoiding drama in relationships is that we all have a tendency to get lost in our own heads. We know ourselves (or rather, we *think* we do) so well and are so familiar with our own wants and needs that we don't realize that we lack a certain degree of self-awareness.

Those less charitable might phrase it differently. "Has their head wedged up their own ass," perhaps.

We focus outward, looking for validation and distraction because… well, it's easier than looking inward. Being alone with our thoughts, examining ourselves and questioning our beliefs — especially beliefs that confirm that we're right — is incredibly uncomfortable. We all have a psychological immune system to maintain our own identity that rejects information that contradicts our sense of self. This is why it's frequently so difficult to recognize that we're often our own worst enemy — the things that make us see ourselves in a bad light are ignored, invalidated or otherwise rationalized away. We don't want to believe we're wrong and we take criticism, even self-directed criticism, as condemnation rather than as an evaluation.

In addition, some people will take the opposite reaction to criticism — they'll martyr themselves to their mistakes, declaring themselves to be the worst, the unforgivable and so forth. This breast-beating, wailing and gnashing of teeth is equally unproductive and is as much of a defense-mechanism; it not only disregards the need to change (because they can't) but derails the matter as they beg for sympathy instead. A willingness to improve doesn't mean that you're broken and flawed. Having made mistakes doesn't mean that you're a bad person. Creating unnecessary drama in a relationship doesn't make you a loser or scum; most of the time you weren't even aware you were doing it. Beating yourself over the head with your awfulness is equally as over-dramatic as refusing to believe you could possibly be the problem.

The key to overcoming this defense mechanism is to learn to accept yourself. Accept that you're imperfect but you can improve. Accept that you are not and can not be objective about yourself and that other people's perspective and opinions can be useful and valuable. Listen to what people have to say with as open a mind as you can, taking it as advice, not as judgement. Surround yourself with people who want you to be better.

You may have been the drama bomb before... that's OK. That's in the past. Accept it. Take responsibility for it. Learn from it.

And when once you do, marvel in how wonderful a drama-proof relationship can be.

---

[1] Or Romeo and Juliet for that matter...

TEN
MOVING IN TOGETHER (WITHOUT GOING NUTS)

Moving in together is one of the biggest milestones

MOVING IN TOGETHER is an incredibly significant milestone in a relationship; it's up there with proposing marriage and starting a family in terms of signaling your commitment and investment. It's also incredibly appealing; splitting the bills 50/50, hot and cold running sex whenever you want it, not having to maintain two households, the thrill of waking up with the man or woman you love in your arms…

It's almost enough to call your honey and tell 'em to start packing their bags, isn't it?

Of course, any dream can turn into a nightmare without warning. You may be expecting the sort of cohabitational bliss that you normally only see in 50's sitcoms, but what you get instead is the roommate from hell. You don't know who this obsessive-compulsive demon is and what he's done with the guy you thought you were shacking up with. The awesome "bangin'-out-on-every-flat-surface-in-the-apartment" sex has turned into "Once a month if the stars are aligned perfectly and there's nothing better on TV." Every conversation is a fight about money, chores or how you spend your free time.

You're just about ready to choke a motherfucker and hope that they technically qualify as a recyclable rather than having to wait for the bulk pick-up at the end of the month. Where did your happy fantasy of living together disappear to?

The unavoidable truth is, moving in together will inevitably change your relationship. You're going to be sharing more than a kitchen and the cable bill, you're going to be sharing your *lives*. So if you're thinking of making the big leap into living together, you want to make sure you're going to do it right.

There aren't any guarantees in life, but following these tips will help you avoid turning your domestic paradise into a single-bedroom nightmare.

Make Sure You're Doing It For The Right Reasons

For a lot of couples, moving in together is something that "just happens". Instead of weighing the pros and cons and making plans in advance, the process of cohabitation occurs in dribs and drabs. It starts with keeping a spare toothbrush at their boyfriend or girlfriend's place. Maybe a spare shirt and pair of underwear, just in case. Or a razor and some toiletries because, hey, you never know, right? Before too long one or the other of you decides, hey, you're half-way there already, might as well pull the trigger on this, right? It'll totally be more convenient for the both of you...

Other times it's a matter of necessity, rather than desire; one of you has suddenly found themselves sans apartment for one reason or another and hey, doesn't make sense to just move in together? After all, you get along alright and you were *probably* move in together anyway. You may as well just move that timetable forward a little bit...

Still other times, you may have entirely different reasons for moving in. *You* may be seeing this as a relationship test, trying out what your long-term relationship will be like when the two of you get married while your partner is thinking that this is a low-emotional-investment way of putting off getting engaged while they desperately look for an exit strategy.

Regardless of which path lead you to this point, it's ended up in the same place: you've not had any conversation about what moving in means or what your expectations are. As a result, the two of you have ideas that are night-and-day different from one another and you're inevitably going to come into conflict when you get clocked upside the head with the hob-nailed boot of reality.

To make matters worse, by the time you've realized that moving in together — or your entire relationship, for that matter — was a mistake, pulling out is much, much harder than it would be if the two of you were still living separately. Your lives – and finances – are so intertwined now that it can feel like you're stuck. Doubly so if you live in a city where affordable living space is rarer than hen's teeth.

You have nowhere to go and your life (and money) is so tied up in your shared home that you can't afford to leave.

If you're going to move in with your honey, you can't just throw your stuff into a couple boxes, carry them over to her place and call it a day. You have to have a long series of conversations to make sure you're both on the same page.

Sort Out The Money Issues First

The first thing that needs to happen before you move in is that you need to have the money conversation. Before you even start *thinking* of buying packing material, you both need to sit down and hash out your financial issues in painstakingly tedious detail. It can be an incredibly awkward conversation to have, especially if there's a significant difference in your financial situations, but it's easily the most important. Money is one of the biggest cause of conflict with couples — single or married — who live together, and poor planning now can haunt you for *decades*.

To start with, whose name is going to be on the lease? If you're both moving into a new place together, is the lease going to be in both of your names? Whichever of you has the better credit rating will probably be the official renter of record. If your girlfriend is moving into your place — or you're moving into hers — the name on the lease is going to make a significant difference. If your boyfriend ends up not coughing up his half of the rent and causing your landlord to begin eviction proceedings, it's *your* credit rating that's going to take the hit. The same applies to who the utilities are registered to. If things go wrong and you're listed as the responsible party, it's *your* ass that's going to be twisting in the wind, no matter how responsible you may have been with your end of things.

While you're at it, how *are* you going to handle bills? Do you both pay your half, or will one of you be responsible for sending the payments in? Will you be establishing a joint checking account that you both pay into? If so, will you *both* have signing privileges? Will one of you be paying the rent while the other handles the utilities? If you're dealing with a metered utility like electricity or — in some cases — Internet access, and one of you is using it far more of the utility in question, do they pay a greater portion? Or are you splitting it down the middle 50/50?

What about insurance? If there's a significant income disparity between the two of you, are you going to be expected to kick in the same amount each month, or does the person with more take-home pay shoulder more of the financial burden?

How about large purchases? If you decide you want that huge flat-screen TV or a new leather couch, do you have the autonomy to just go ahead and buy it, or are you going to have to work things out in advance?

These are questions that you need to ask and answer long before you start looking at moving in.

Pro tip: most banks can set up automatic bill payments via their websites. Take advantage of this service. Knowing that your bills will be paid on time automatically even if you can't remember what day it is will save you both a lot of headaches.

Establish the Ground Rules In Advance (And Negotiate Everything)

Living together is completely different from staying together over long weekends. One of the hardest parts of making the transition from "single" to "part of a couple" is making your lives mesh neatly. We all have our own set routines and ways of doing things and trying to adapt to others' methods often confuses and frustrates us. Once you no longer have your own territory to retreat to, you're inevitably going to discover that the way *you* are used to living may not be completely compatible with the way your partner used to and vice versa. You're a neat-freak who likes keeping your place as tidy and organized as possible while they're used to living in an apartment where the cockroaches moved out in order to find a place that's less down-market.

Much like dealing with finances, you need to find a way to make your lifestyles mesh as smoothly as possible… *before* you're committed to a lease. More often than not, what we end up with is a mishmash unspoken responsibilities and duties that are somehow as binding as a signed contract. Instead of trying to sort out who does what, we often just fall into our roles without comment, assuming that the other person has no problem taking the position we've functionally dumped on them. Sometimes it works… sometimes it doesn't. And when it *doesn't* work, then you end up butting heads more and more often and your relationship starts to resemble a cold war between two super-powers. This isn't good for *anyone*. After all, you don't want to be the couple who doesn't fight about the dishes so much as play intense games of "Fungus Chicken", do you?

Instead, you want to start to negotiate who is responsible for what. In some cases, one of you will be a more natural fit for the role. If you prefer things to be cleaned thus so, then you're more likely to be in charge of cleaning. If your partner has very strong opinions about food, then odds are they'll gravitate towards doing most of the cooking. In other cases, you'll want to split things up or trade responsibilities in one area for a concession in another. Compromise will be the name of the game here. Splitting up the chores in advance means that you can ensure that neither of you is left feeling like an indentured servant, drudging away to a chorus of singing cartoon mice while your honey is busy in the other room catching up on *Doctor Who* reruns and Internet porn. Laying out the responsibilities early means that you can ensure that everybody is pulling their weight, rather than unfairly stacking the deck.

Don't assume that everything has to be exactly equal; even in the most egalitarian relationships, somebody is inevitably going to end up shouldering more of the burden in one area or the other. Sometimes one partner or the other has no problem, say, doing all the housework as long as the other does the lion's share of some other household task.

However, this negotiation goes beyond just who's supposed to do which household chores. Living together means that your habits now affect somebody else; not adjusting your routine because "this is the way things I've always done things" has caused more fights and break-ups than I can count. This is why you want to have a detailed negotiation about almost *every* aspect of your living together: what do you expect, what are you used to, what can you simply not stand and what are you willing to be flexible about? What time will the two of you be having dinner on most nights? Is one person responsible for breakfast, or do you both just do your own thing in the morning? Are you going to want to be spending some quality time playing *Overwatch* every day? Are they going to want to be able to go to their regular "drinks with the guys after work" like they have been? When you get home from work, are you going to need time to decompress before you're able to face another human?

Will it be awkward? Yeah, probably. We're not used to having trying to communicate our specific emotional or physical needs so bluntly. It can feel weird to just state that you prefer cuddling on the couch to making out or that she views talking over unpausable cutscenes in video games as being cause for murder. It can be uncomfortable actually trying to give a voice to something we usually only feel. But that lack of communication is going to cause more problems than just feeling a little awkward, so the sooner you can work things through, the better it will be for you.

And don't forget: you can and should renegotiate frequently. Circumstances change, lifestyles adjust; a relationship is an ongoing conversation and should be treated like one.

Be Ready To Redecorate

Living together means you need to make your new place feel like home to both of you. If you're going to both be happy and feel comfortable in your new apartment, you have to make sure you both have a mutual sense of ownership. When one person has dominated the decor of the house or apartment and you only have a handful of touches that show you live there too, you can feel like you're functionally a second-class citizen in your own home.

This is especially true if you're moving into your partner's place or they're moving into yours. If you want them to feel as though they actually have a place there instead of being a long-term guest, this means that you're going to have to do more than just give them space on the book-shelf and room for a couple dishes in the cabinet. You want your home to be a *blend* of your two personalities rather than one dominant theme with the occasional hint that maybe somebody else lives there too.

This is easy in theory, but often surprisingly difficult in practice. Letting somebody else have a say in the decor of your living space is incredibly intimate and can be challenging to your identity. If the two of you disagree on a particular piece of furniture, it can feel like you're being judged on a deep and personal level. At the same time, you may discover the things you *think* are important mean less to you than you realize and that things you always took for granted are actually incredibly important. It's astounding how often you discover that some random tchotchke you haven't thought about in years actually has profound sentimental meaning to you until your snuggle-bunny is suggesting that maybe you box it up and put it into storage.

At the end of the day, this means that you need to be ready for a great deal of compromise and sacrifice for the both of you. You may love that reclining lounge chair with the pulsating shiatsu massage and built in mini-fridge, but living together means having to give it up so that your girlfriend can put in her couch and ottoman combo instead. In exchange, as much as she loves Louis XII replicas, she has to be willing to compromise on the Shaker modern style furniture instead.

If you're lucky enough to have the space, then it can help to have an area where each of you have absolute dominion over the decor, while other areas are a melding of your sensibilities. It's easier to give someone greater leeway in the living room if you can have your private office or control over every aspect of the kitchen.

Have Separate Bathroom Sinks

Just trust me on this one. If it's at all possible, you want his and her sinks and mirrors in the bathroom. You will never fight more often or more viciously than when it comes to getting space in the bathroom counter.

Hell, aim for separate entire bathrooms if you can. This may well save your relationship and your *life*.

Be Prepared For Your Relationship To Change

Living together means that changes to your relationship are inevitable. Even couples who've dated for *years* prior to living together will go through the long and sometimes torturous routine of learning all of their honey-bunny's little quirks and habits. The little things that were cute while you weren't up in each other's business all day and all night will become teeth-grindingly annoying. Snuggling together and waking up wrapped in each other's arms starts to become less romantic when you're sucking in his morning breath and he's realizing that you fart like the brass section of a John Williams retrospective in your sleep. She'll resent the pubic hair on the toilet rim, you'll want to know why you suddenly don't have any space on the bathroom sink. The little things that you used to be able to laugh off will cause you to pull your hair out as you resist the urge to blow your top.

That 24-hour sex-a-thon you were expecting will also dry up... likely sooner than you expect. When you're living separately, you have to make time for sex; you only have so much time together so you have to make the most efficient (and squishy) use of it that you can. When you have all the time in the world, carving out naked time becomes that much less important. There will be nights when all the two of you will want to do is collapse on the couch, watch *The Flash* and turn your brains off.... sex will be the last thing on your mind. Living together means that you will start to take sex for granted. It's like having your favorite movie on all day, every day – it's great at first, but eventually you're going to get bored of it and then it will become the background noise of your life as you start focusing on everything else.

The survival of your relationship after you move in together will require effort on both of your parts. The two of you will have to put more work in than you expect – not just to adjusting to your new life together but also keeping your relationship fresh and exciting.

Don't let the challenges intimidate you. Living together is a momentous step in the course of a relationship... but it's one that can lead to some of the best times and fondest memories of your lives.

ELEVEN

GETTING SPACE IN A RELATIONSHIP

There's Such A Thing As Too Much Togetherness

THERE ARE CERTAIN phrases that chill the marrow when you hear them in the context of a relationship. "We need to talk," of course, is the great grand-daddy of them all, along with "where do you see this going?". But few phrases ring in our ears like a banshee's wail foretelling the death of a relationship like "I need some space." We hear that phrase and translate it as "I'm working up the guts to dump your sorry ass."

Except… that's always not the case. In fact, the phrase "I need some space" highlights one of the most common misconceptions about relationships.

One of the things that people often don't understand about relationships is that everybody needs their space at one point or another. We have a tendency to treat our romantic relationships like starring in *The Defiant Ones*: once you've agreed that you're in a relationship, you are now shackled together for all time, never to be alone again and the only thing you can do is learn how to work around it.

You're no longer an individual, you see; you're now officially a couple – a gestalt entity forming feet and legs, arms and body that somehow still has a hard time deciding what to watch on Netflix, never mind agreeing which of you forms the head. This is especially true when you are young and/or new to relationships in general – spending every waking moment together is seen as proof of just how much you love one another and why you're so perfect together.

But that's not how people work. You don't subsume your identity into the collective Matrix that is your union, exchanging your sense of self for a cutesy portmanteau couple-name that even TMZ would gag over. Just because you love somebody doesn't mean that your need for time to yourself goes away, and wanting time to do your own thing with your friends doesn't mean that your love is any less "real" or "true". For that matter, spending every single minute of every single day together doesn't mean that your relationship is wonderful and all cartoon birds and rainbows and hot and cold running blow-jobs.

In fact, by not making room for having some "me" time, you're actually hurting your relationship. So let's talk a little about just how you can have space in your relationship without sacrificing intimacy.

Everybody Needs Their Space… Even You

One of the most counterintuitive parts of relationship maintenance is that having space is actually critical to the success of lasting relationships. In fact, according to an ongoing federal study, having space and privacy is as important as a good sex life – if not more so. Ensuring that you both have time apart is a key component to a happy, satisfied relationship. Taking some time to yourself allows you to recharge your emotional batteries, connect with friends on your own and keep feeling like you have your own life... even though you now share it with someone else.

Part of the problem is that we often define ourselves by our relationships. We assume a new identity – often one that replaces our own; we're now "X's boyfriend" or "Y's wife", and that can leave us feeling trapped without a sense of "self".

By having space to do your own thing and pursue your own interests, you're able be an individual again, not just part of a whole. It means that you have an opportunity to do things strictly for yourself and give you that sense of autonomy again. It also allows you to pursue your interests and hobbies without having to drag your partner along for the ride; there's nothing that kills the joy of doing something you love like forcing somebody who only *barely* tolerates it to take part. In fact, there are relationship experts who go so far as to advocate taking separate *vacations*; after all, one person's relaxing disconnect from all modern media in the middle of nowhere is another person's vision of Hell.

Getting space lets you have a sense of privacy — a need that doesn't go away just because you're in a relationship with someone, by the way — and feelings of autonomy and self-determination. You get time off to relax without feeling as though you're neglecting the responsibilities of being part of a couple. For introverts, it can be a way of recharging one's emotional batteries; just because you love someone doesn't mean that they can't be draining on you. This can be especially important if you're an introvert who's dating an extrovert — the extroverted partner's need for company can be exhausting.

Just as important, however, it helps take the pressure off us and our partners to be the only source of each other's emotional and social support. No matter how much you love somebody, they can't be all things to all people – and neither can you. One of the biggest causes of emotional strain in relationships is the feeling of being solely responsible for your partner's emotional needs. That is an intense amount of pressure to put on somebody, even somebody you love to distraction, and it can be exhausting being the sole pillar of support. Taking time to yourself allows you both to foster connections with other people and widen your base of emotional support – taking the weight off of one person's shoulders and leaving them feeling less overwhelmed.

Understanding The Different Needs For Space

One thing to keep in mind is that everyone has very different needs for space and alone-time. The obvious example are introverts and extroverts. Introverts recharge their emotional energy through solitary pursuits while extroverts get their energy through being around other people. As a result, the introvert is going to have a greater need for space than the extrovert.

But the need for space doesn't just divide along lines of extroversion or introversion; more often than not it comes down to a mix of personality, feeling secure in the relationship and in the opportunities for personal time. In studies, women often tend to be the ones who complain about not having as much space or opportunity for solo time as men. In its own way, it's not terribly surprising; on average, women tend still tend to shoulder the majority of the caregiving responsibilities with children and providing emotional labor in hetero relationships. Couple this with jobs and housework — even when household duties are split between partners — and there just tend to not be enough hours in the day to get everything done *and* have time to themselves.

When negotiating to meet one another's need for space in a relationship, it's important to understand the underlying reasons for *wanting* that space. Sometimes it's a matter of fear; someone who craves space may fear over-investing in a relationship and being hurt, while someone who has very little need for space may have anxiety around feeling abandoned. Or it may be that one person wants time to pursue interests that their partner doesn't necessarily share or like; giving them their time alone lets them feel that they aren't giving up something they love in the name of a relationship — a guaranteed recipe for resentment. Or it just may be that they're feeling suffocated and need time to blow off steam and come back after some time to remind themselves that they're an individual as well as part of a couple. Understanding the reason for that alone time helps you and your partner to accept that your need for space isn't a referendum on them or your relationship — it's simply part of who you are.

And it's important that both partners feel they are getting their needs for alone time met because otherwise they'll *make* that space… by becoming more and more emotionally distant, leading to the eventual break-up.

The Many Ways of Getting Space

There are a multitude of ways of meeting your need for space in a relationship, depending on whether you're looking for alone time or wanting to spend time with your friends. A regularly scheduled event such as a poker night, a tabletop gaming session or amateur sports league can be a way of getting your space and maintaining your relationship with your social circle. Other ways include going to movies on your own, going for walks or drives or other activities that get you out of the house and on your own for a while.

At the extreme end of these options is for you and your partner to take the aforementioned separate vacations — something a number of experts recommend, in fact. While this can sound like a precursor to a break-up, separate vacations can be a surprising benefit to your relationship. Not only does it mean that you have greater flexibility on where to go and what to do — you may want to go hiking in the Grand Canyon while your partner would rather spend a week being a tourist in New York City — but having those separate experiences can actually bring some much needed novelty and newness to your relationship together. Having new stories and experiences to share helps counterbalance the malaise of "they've told this story thirty times before." Traveling with your friends can also give the opportunity to spend time with and renew your bond bond with your bros or sestras in ways that you often can't when you're in a relationship.

But not all ways of getting alone time require leaving the city… or even the house. Carving out some space in your house or apartment for yourself can help serve as a retreat when you need time alone. If you have the room, these can be literal, physical spaces that the two of you could designate as your own private retreats; a man-cave, workshop, craft room or library/office that you could decorate and trick out however you want. Detached garages and spare bedrooms make for excellent personal spaces if you have them available.

However, personal space and distance in the relationship can be as much in the mind as anything else. It's possible to have *emotional* space, even when your partner is 20 feet away. Having an opportunity to just chill out on the couch and binge on episodes of *Daredevil* and *Bojack Horseman* without being bothered, to hole up in the bedroom and listen to podcasts for a couple hours can make the difference between feeling trapped and having your needs met. Closing the door, turning on Spotify and soaking away in the tub for an hour or two without being disturbed is just as useful if space is at a premium. Having a place where you can take a time out and just relax on your own can be invaluable, especially when you both feel as though someone's always right on top of you at all times. The ability to have a brief escape from the stress of living together — and it *will* be stressful at times — can mean the difference between screaming matches and connubial bliss.

However you do it, carving out space for yourselves is a critical part of staying together. Taking the time to yourself to recharge your emotional batteries and do some self-maintenance as an individual makes it much easier to spend time together as a happy, excited couple.

Communicate, Communicate, Communicate

Finding ways of meeting your need for space requires you to communicate with your partner... and that can often be the problem. We tend not to talk about our need for space until it has already reached a boiling point. At that point, we're not exactly in the best mindset to explain that there's nothing wrong with the relationship and wanting to go away for a weekend by ourselves doesn't mean we're having an affair. Ideally, the best time to talk about one's need for space is early in the relationship, when you're still establishing the new patterns that will define how you spend time together. This is especially true if you're planning on moving in together. It's one thing when you have your own place to retreat to. It's another entirely when you're now sharing a one-bedroom apartment and there's no real sanctum sanctorum for you to decompress. Everyone has a set amount of distance that they need before they feel like they're "alone" and this can be difficult to manage when your entire home is shared space.

Again: this doesn't mean that you don't love your partner or that you're incompatible on some fundamental level. It's a simple truth about *anyone*, be they rats or humans: you can only be crammed into a tiny space together[1] for so long before "I love you" becomes "I will *kill* you and no jury on this earth will convict me."

When you're explaining your needs, one of the worst things you can say is simply "I need some space." This is entirely too general and vague. *You* may think that you're just expressing a need for private time, but *she* is hearing that you're sick of her and want time away because you're distancing yourself in preparation for a break-up. Instead, you should explain what you want and why. Being specific eliminates much of the anxiety that asking for space can cause in your partner. When you're explaining what you want with concrete examples, it doesn't feel like you're unhappy or looking for the exit. You may say "I need time to recharge," or "I want some time to just be by myself" or "I want to spend time with my friends" or even "I just need to decompress so I'm going to binge on some *Bravely Default* for the next couple hours, please don't bother me unless something is actively on fire" — these are all about something you need for *yourself* instead of conveying the message that the problem is with your relationship. Be specific — do you need an hour or two chilling at the library? An afternoon? A day? Explain what you're going to do as well and where – you're not conducting an affair, running a meth ring or spying on your nation's enemies, you're just carving out time for yourself.

It can be especially helpful to schedule your time in advance; this way you're not going to be needing your space just as your partner's expecting you to help run the cat out to her appointment at the vet or doing the much-needed yard work. This allows the two of you to work around your respective needs and reach a compromise that still means you are spending quality time as a couple as well. After all, as important as having your alone time can be, having couple time is just as important; too much space goes from needing personal time to "avoidance" and ends up weakening the relationship. There are reasons why some of the loneliest people out there are actually married and live with their spouse; their lives have become entirely separate, despite sharing the same house. One of them may spend all their time on their phone or tablet in one room while the other occupies the TV in another, rarely sharing any time together at all.

Get your space and your "me" time… but just remember to not sacrifice all of the "we" time to do so.

---

[1] Incidentally, I will be offering relationship counseling services for the various stars of "Small House Hunters"…

PART THREE:
TROUBLESHOOTING YOUR RELATIONSHIP

So, fair warning: this section is going to be a bit of a downer. It may also be *the* most important section of the book.

I'm not going to lie to you: every relationship is going to have it's ups and downs and sometimes those downs can be pretty damn deep. There will be times when you're going to have to face down situations that will make you question whether or not this relationship still has a chance… or if you even *want* to keep it going.

Infidelity, in particular, is something you very well may have to deal with. Traditional monogamy is hard to execute perfectly, and the longer the two of you are together, the greater the likelihood that one or both of you may stray.

However, it's in acknowledging these potential problems that we're able to overcome them. By learning to recognize the relationship danger signs, you're better able to fix them before they get so great that you've passed the point of no return. Other times, it may be that realization that this relationship has come to it's natural conclusion - or that you need to get out *now*.

Don't worry, this isn't all gloom and doom. Things may feel bleak, but there's a lot here about how to *save* your relationship, not just mourn it's passing.

So grit your teeth and let's do this thing.

TWELVE

BEWARE THE RELATIONSHIP DANGER SIGNS

Are You Heading Towards a Breakup?

OVER THE COURSE of your love life, you're going to have to deal with a breakup. Sometimes you'll see the breakup coming a mile away like an oncoming train and you'll realize that there's no getting around it. It's going to happen and the only thing left to do is to brace yourself and try to figure out how to make it not suck as much.

But then there are the breakups that sneak up on you and hit you when you're not looking. There's nothing that delivers a nut-kick to your soul like a breakup that seems to come screaming out of the clear blue sky. These are the ones that just explode around you and leave you blinking and wide-eyed in the crater that used to be your life, wondering what the hell happened.

But while it may hit you out of the blue, breakups rarely happen in a vacuum. If you want to pull your relationship back from the brink, you want to keep an eye out for these warning signs that you're headed to a breakup.

Danger Sign #1: You Fight A Lot. Like, a lot

As I've already told you, fights are going happen. If you're dating another person, there's going to be conflict. If you have two (or more) people, there's going to be an inevitable clash of opinions, desires and interests. The only way you're not going to have a fight with your significant other is if they're an inanimate object.

But there are fights and there are *fights*. There are times when you're just two passionate people whose primary mode of communication is to explode like Vesuvius and then wrap around each other like lovesick octopuses dressed like Japanese schoolgirls. The fights flare up like swamp gas and then they're forgotten like a fart in a windstorm. Other times there are legitimate issues within a relationship that need to be resolved.

And then there are times when the two of you are just coasting from conflict to conflict, where those moments of peace are really just the calm before next storm.

Anything could set off the next explosion, no matter how banal; one minute you're trying to figure out where you want to eat and the next you're screaming at each other about the thing that one of you said three months ago. You're pissed at them, they're pissed at you and it seems like everybody's just looking for more reasons to be upset at everyone else.

How Do You Pull This Back from A Breakup?

You have to break the cycle. This can be shockingly hard to do;

after all, when you've hit a pattern of fight after fight, you become far more invested in proving that you were the one who was in the right all along. You've been saving up slights and grievances to whip out at a moment's notice like the world's bitterest game of Uno.

It's that very sense of your own wounded pride that's screwing you over. The two of you have gotten *so* invested in the fighting and the point scoring that you've long lost track of what triggered those fights. Now you're not arguing over your issues, you're fighting because you've *been* fighting. Each new dust up and conflagration just rips the scabs off the wounds from the *last* fight... and usually reopens a few scars for good measure.

If you want to make this relationship work — assuming it can be saved at all — *one* of you has to be the first to stop fighting, and start listening. In all likelihood that means *you*, because, frankly, if you're waiting for your partner to do it, you're going to be waiting for a damn long time. There's a natural tendency towards defensiveness and trying to protect your ego, because it's *really* damn hard to let all of those insults and accusations slide. It's even *harder* if it means accepting that maybe you were the asshole. It's entirely possible that yes, you are the less-wrong[1] of the two of you. Backing down without having that acknowledged can be a bitter pill to swallow. But you have to ask yourself: is being "right" going to make you feel better when your partner's gone? Is it going to keep you company in those lonely nights afterwards? If you genuinely want to fix things, then you need to be willing to be the first to put up your sword as a gesture of good faith.

Swallow your pride, de-escalate and try to assess what the real issue is instead of one-upping each other in moral indignation.

But while we're talking about fights...

Danger Sign #2: You Keep Having The Same Argument Over and Over Again

Sometimes it's not the frequency of the fights that's the problem. Sometimes it's what you're fighting about.

One of the surest signs that you're heading towards a breakup is when the same issue comes up over and over and over. After a while, it's like you're stuck in the world's shittiest time loop; the circumstances may change but you're always ending up in the same place over and over again, and once you think it's over, it comes up again. You try things differently each time but somehow you always end up circling back to that same fight you've been having.

Sometimes it comes up as a suggestion. Other times it's a discussion. Still other times, it's a knock down, drag out, "why won't you listen to me already?" fight. The lyrics may change, but the song is the same and you know every beat and measure by heart. Part of what makes this particular breakup warning sign insidious is how often the inciting incident seems like it shouldn't be that big of a deal; as a result, the breakup ends up catching you off guard.

But no matter how unimportant it may seem to you, the more often this issue comes up, the closer and closer you come to watching your relationship fall apart.

How Do You Pull This Back from A Breakup?

The fact that the issue keeps coming up is because it's never been resolved.

Duh.

The thing you need to confront is *why* it's never been resolved. Maybe you think it's something stupid and you brush it off. Maybe you think your partner's being unreasonable or that nothing could possibly satisfy them. Or maybe you're the sort of person who will just say whatever it takes to make them drop the subject.

Well guess what? No amount of passive-aggressiveness coating is going to turn this particular grit into a pearl, which means that the only way this breakup can be avoided is to face the issue head on. You're going to have to sit down and actually hash things out... and the first step is going to be making sure you actually *understand* what your partner's asking for. More often than not, the surface reason for the fight is merely the latest symptom of the underlying disease; focusing on that specific issue — as many people do — means that you're not actually treating the real problem. If you get too caught up in the specifics, then you end up seeming like you're *deliberately* missing the point and disrespecting your partner in the process. This is one of those times when real communication is going to make a difference; if you're just assuming that you understand, then odds are good that you're missing the problem for the symptom.

After all: if you were dealing with the real issue, then you'd have resolved things already.

Now in fairness: it's not going to always be you who's the problem[2]. Sometimes it really is a case of your partner stepping on a particular landmine over and over again. If that's what's happening here, then ask yourself if you've been as clear as you can be about communicating your *real* issue, rather than whatever triggered the fight *this* time?

And while you're at it, you're going to have to cultivate some self-awareness – is this a case of your partner legitimately being unreasonable, or do you just not want to do whatever it is you need to do to fix things? Do you mean well and forget to start making changes you've promised — in which case you need to start building a system to make sure you remember — or do you just "forget"?

Danger Sign #3: You're Not Having Sex Any More (And You're Not Enjoying The Sex You Have)

One of the biggest, flashing signs that a breakup is in your future is that the sex sucks... if you're having it at all.

Sexual satisfaction and sexual compatibility are key components of a lasting and happy relationship. Sex, after all, is one of the key ways we share intimacy, display affection and cement the emotional bonds that bring us together and keep us together. When we're not satisfied — either because we're not having enough (or any) sex or because the sex is boring, unenjoyable or unpleasant — then that dissatisfaction seeps into other aspects of our relationship as well. We start to resent our partners for not meeting our needs or for subjecting us to something that we dislike. Other forms of intimacy start to dwindle and fall away, increasing that sense of distance between us.

And of course, we may end up cheating on our partners and turning a potential breakup into an inevitability instead.

Once the sex goes, the relationship soon follows... unless you can pull it back out of the downward spiral.

How Do You Pull This Back from A Breakup?

It all comes down to why the sex is bad or non-existent.

One of the most common reasons why sex fades in a relationship is because people get bored. Just as it's possible to fall into a rut in your day to day relationships, it's possible to fall into a rut, sexually. Part of the issue is, shockingly, how we tend to view sex in committed relationships – especially marriage – versus sex with relative strangers. We're taught over and over again that kinky, crazy sexual adventures are for the young and uncommitted; once we're "in love", married or gasp old1 it's time to put it all away and go back to basic vanilla sex. Even 50 Shades of Grey tells people that sexual adventure is great at first, but the goal should be to put it all behind you and just enjoy basic missionary instead. Doubly so if you have kids; you don't put the mother of your children in a bondage harness and suspend her from the ceiling, for Christ's sake!

The other reason that sex tends to fade is that we're not having the sex we enjoy or that we're not enjoying the sex we're having… but at the same time, it's incredibly hard to tell your partner that. No matter how well intentioned or carefully phrased, hearing that someone doesn't like the sex you're having is a major blow to the ego – especially if it's been going on for quite some time.

The key to fixing all of this? It's two-fold. The first is: communication, communication, communication. It's one thing to try to inject novelty into the bedroom by, say, bringing a soft rope and a silk blindfold, but if the problem isn't that you're bored but that you don't like the sex you're having, nothing's going to get better. If you're having sex with someone, you need to be able comfortable talking about sex with them – both to advocate for your pleasure but also to help fulfill theirs. If you can't talk to your partner about what you want and don't want, and if your partner can't do the same with you, there's no room to change and improve.

The other part that it takes to fix a flagging sexual relationship? Embracing the concept of being what sex advice columnist and official

NerdLove Celebrity Patronus Dan Savage calls GGG: being Good (in bed), Giving (as a lover) and Game (for trying new things for your partner within reason). That third G is often what trips partners up. Many people have kinks or interests that they may be hesitant to bring up for fear of being rejected by their partner. Similarly, if you're not necessarily into something that your partner is, it's going to be much harder to want to fulfill that desire or kink; you may well feel bothered by the fact that you were asked to do this. As a result: nobody's happy. One partner's needs are going unfulfilled, with a bonus serving of rejection and shame while the other is feeling weirded out by their partner's desires.

But there's actual science to back up the benefit of being GGG. Studies have found that couples who have greater sexual communal (that is, a willingness to stretch to meet their partners needs) strength have both greater sexual satisfaction in general[3] but also greater sexual desire over time[4]. The benefits to the relationship goes beyond just someone's very particular itch being scratched; that feeling of being appreciated by one's partner and that they're willing to work to meet your needs (and vice versa) is validating. And those benefits go both ways – being willing to try things you may not necessarily be interested makes you feel better as well.

Danger Sign #4: Your Lives Are Going In Very Different Directions

One of the best parts of a relationship is building your future together. In an ideal world, this person is your partner-in-crime, the person who you know you're going to love even when the two of you are broken down and decrepit and arguing about who's turn it is to have their adult diapers changed.

Over time however, you realize that you both have incredibly divergent ideas of what your future entails. You're excited to pick out the names of your future children… but she's realizing that she doesn't want kids. Ever. You're a driven, ambitious professional and he can't be bothered to look for work because he's needs the time to "work on his music". Or "write his novel." Or any number of excuses. They seemed plausible – even charming – when you first started but now you're worried that you've tethered yourself to a slacker who's going to be holding you back.

Of course, it needn't be as dramatic as fights over having children or how many. It could be as simple as where the two of you will live, or your where you are with your careers. Where are the two of you going to live: the big city? The suburbs? A house in the middle of nowhere? Are you willing — or able, for that matter — to pull up stakes if your significant other gets an offer for her dream job that requires moving across the country? Or worse: half-way around the globe?

Do you have the same views on religion? If the two of you aren't of the same faith, are you going to be able to find an accord between them? What if you have kids?

Everyone's familiar with the idea that opposites attract, but in reality, if you're *too* different, those differences are going to end up being a massive strain on your relationship. As much as you may even genuinely love each other, the cold hard fact is that sometimes being in love just isn't enough to make a relationship work.

How Do You Pull This Back From a Break Up?

To be perfectly honest, this one is the hardest to pull back from. There comes a point when differences can be just so irreconcilable that the only way to preserve the emotional core of your relationship —

that love and affection you have for one another — is to break up.

But difficult doesn't mean impossible. In this case, however, it means being willing to make a number of sacrifices and compromises.

The younger you are, the easier it is to be flexible. The life you see for yourself — especially when you're still in college or fresh out in the world — isn't necessarily the one that you may end up in, or even *want*. Often, what we *think* we want falls away when we're confronted with the reality of it. Other times, you'll find that your expectations and dreams have changed as you've grown and matured. At times like those, you maw well realize that you're holding onto those old dreams out of habit or nostalgia rather than any desire to make them happen.

Regardless, before you pull the trigger on a break-up, you need to take some time to think about just how firmly you're committed to your current life... and whether you're willing to make some sacrifices in the name of your relationship. Is your life in a position where you could put certain aspects of it on hold, if only for a little while? Would you be able to pursue your own goals if you moved? Which do you prioritize more: your career path or building a family? Don't let the idea that you *have* to choose "family" or be a selfish jerk sway you if you're not the parenting type; *not* having kids is just as valid a life choice as the 3.5 kids and the white picket fence in the suburbs.

It's that willingness to make the effort that's the most important. It's one thing to see that you're headed towards a breakup. But if you want to save your relationship, you have to do more than recognize the warning signs – you have to put in the work to change it's course.

––––––––––––––––––––

[1] Notice how carefully I *don't* say "right"

[2] By necessity, I have to focus on the actions of the reader, after all…

[3] http://nrdlv.co/2ajMBfm

[4] http://nrdlv.co/2aiT00u

THIRTEEN
IS YOUR RELATIONSHIP TOXIC?

The Dangers of the Toxic Relationship

I REALIZE THAT it's a little odd to talk about recognizing and getting out of toxic relationships in a book that's ostensibly about making a relationship *work*.

Thing is: sometimes the problem isn't with the relationship, it's who you're in the relationship *with*. There will be times where nothing you do will actually *fix* things because the issue is that you're in a relationship with someone who's an abusive, emotional vampire.

It can be hard to recognize when you're in a toxic relationship; you may have to rely on the perspective of others to clue you in to the situation. Your friends will often have a different view on what's going on than you do.

And they will want to share those thoughts with you if you give them half a chance.

Believe me, there are few things more frustrating than watching a good friend of yours in a horrible relationship. No matter what you say or the advice you give, they seem to have all of the emotional survival instincts of a depressed sea captain, determinedly going down with (and on) the HRMS Douchebag all the way to the bottom of the Atlantic.

I should know. My friends love reminding me about mine.

Back in the bad old days, I was notoriously prone for my poor-decision skills when it came to women and relationships. I was a bubbling stew of low self-esteem, a defeatist attitude towards dating and the dogged belief that I couldn't do any better, and that was never more evident than in the way I related to the opposite sex. If I wasn't chasing after women because I thought I could get what I wanted from them (i.e. sex) without giving a damn about how it might affect them, I was enduring relationships with women I should have long broken up with because I thought... well, because I didn't know any better.

It was a period of extreme frustration for my friends and family because they felt so damn helpless watching me piss my self-worth away and not knowing how to wake me up to what was really going on. At the risk of quoting song lyrics, when a man thinks he loves a woman, he tends to be willing to overlook a *lot*... and I was willing to overlook the fact that I was fucking miserable. I had convinced myself that I was in love with the woman I was dating – and to an extent, I was – and that meant that I was willfully blind to just how bad the relationship was and how much damage it was doing to me and to my friends. Part of it was, admittedly, because I thought that this was the best that I could do but another part was the fact that I just couldn't see how toxic my relationship with this woman had become.

After all, like the poet says: the more you suffer, the more it shows you really care, right?

Yeah.[1]

I spent years in complete misery because I couldn't see the signs that my relationship had turned to poison... and everybody knew it but me.

Ever since then, I've seen far too many people caught in the same relationship death-spiral that I was, blind to just how bad things were and convinced that maybe this was just how relationships were supposed to be. So in hopes of opening a few eyes, I give you 5 signs that you're stuck in a toxic relationship.

They Undermine You At Every Opportunity

One of the first signs that you're in a toxic relationship is fairly simple: you can never get your legs under you because your partner'll kick them out from under you every chance they get.

You dread hanging out with your significant other and her friends because you know that it's going to be a non-stop parade of jokes... most of them at your expense. No matter what you do, somehow you become the punch-line of every joke and insult that gets flung about. Even a compliment gets followed up with another put-down because hey, can't let you get a swelled head, now right?

Of course, you can't complain about it because all that means is that you're just a wuss who can't take a joke. Be careful, we don't want to hurt their *widdle feewings*, gang!

Other times, it'll be that you can't talk about your plans because all you'll hear is about how you're going to screw it up. You'll get a never-ending parade of your mistakes, failures and other ways you've fucked up. It's not that they're trying to *hurt* you, but he's the only person who'll give it to you *straight* and he just doesn't want you to get hurt or be disappointed after all...

There's seemingly nothing you can do without getting a ration of shit from someone who's supposed to be your partner; there's rarely a moment where they *don't* take the opportunity to get in a dig at your insecurities or perceived flaws. It may be said with a smile and a nudge, but it's almost always at a time when you're feeling good. Or around other people. Or at times when maybe you need a little reassurance from someone who supposedly cares for you.

Everything you do is subject to constant criticism. No topic is off limits or too personal to be brought up at the most embarrassing or awkward times possible. But hey, it's all in good fun, right? It's just banter. It's all for your own good. He's trying to help you, after all.

It's one thing when you and your honey playfully give each other shit.

It's another entirely when they seem to take every possible opportunity to cut you down.

There are plenty of relationships out there that seemingly thrive on a playfully antagonistic vibe but there's an undercurrent of genuine love and affection and the awareness that there are distinct limits. For all that you may enjoy needling or teasing each other, your partner in a relationship is just that: your partner. They're the one who is supposed to have your back no matter what, not the one making the point of cutting your legs out from under you whenever they get the chance.

They Suck The Life Out Of You

One of the surest signs of a toxic relationship is often one of the hardest to recognize in yourself… but odds are good your friends will have seen it.

You may have been lively and outgoing once, but lately it just seems like you don't have any energy. At all. Every day, you've been waking up at an all-time low and just getting even more drained by the end of the day. You're brewing your coffee with Red Bull but you just can't muster up the energy to be interested in *anything* besides just getting through the day and you just can't put your finger on the reason why.

All of your friends can, though. They may not have said anything — or, just as likely, they *did* say something but you didn't want to hear it — but they've all seen how you're your old self when you're rolling solo, but become a different person when you're with your hunnybun. If your friends can get you out on your own, you're happier, more engaged and more alive. But when your partner is nearby, you just... deflate. You're quieter. You seem subdued. You mouth insists that no, you're having a good time, but your slumped posture and monosyllable answers are telling an entirely different story.

Even when she's out of town, there's no escape. You're acting like your old self again and having a good time... right up until your cell starts to ring and you know letting it go to voicemail just means an even bigger ration of shit to deal with later. So you pick up and everybody around gets to watch all the life drain out of you like a leaky balloon. You're using so much emotional energy dealing with your partner and the stress your relationship causes that you have virtually none left for yourself afterwards.

Your partner is almost *literally* draining the life out of you. It takes all the energy you have to just not give them anything to be mad at you about... and there's *always* something to be mad over. You spend so much time watching your every move, weighing every single word you say and getting ready for the next explosion that you don't have the time or energy for anything else. And frankly, the odds are good they're happier that way. Some people thrive on the attention, on the emotional charge of conflict and and drama, and all that energy's gotta come from somewhere, right?

If even the thought of them leaves you feeling emotionally exhausted, it's time to plan your exit strategy.

It's All About Control

Relationships are supposed to be 50-50, but somehow you and your girlfriend always end up doing what she wants.

To be sure, even the most egalitarian relationships won't always break down perfectly to 50-50. There will always be one partner who's more dominant than the other. But there's one person who direct things, then there's the times when your opinions and interests better match up with your partners'... *or else.*

The slightest concession to something you might want is a massive sacrifice, with all the attending pomp, production, grousing and resigned passive-aggressive sighing that this implies... but if *you* don't give in to what *she* wants, then you're staring down the crater into an emotional Krakatoa. It doesn't matter how reasonable your refusal might be, how minute your hesitation is or how basic your disagreement; the fact that you're not in absolute lockstep with her is the crime that is too great to be forgiven and she will *make sure* that you understand how horrible you are for feeling the way you do.

When you're in a relationship with a toxic person, dissent isn't to be tolerated — and dissent can range from "we disagree on where to eat," to "I thought we agreed that you weren't going to hang out with X/ watch Y/ do Z any more," It doesn't matter that your agreement was under duress. He has a whole host of techniques to bend you to his will and she wields them with the precision and glee of a KGB interrogator trying to wring secrets from an CIA agent.

She may use her affection as both the carrot and the stick. Do what she wants and she'll be lovey-dovey for a little… but give her the slightest bit of resistance and you've been exiled to the snowy wastes of a sexual Siberia until such time as you've shown her that you've suffered enough and repent of all your sins against her. Other times he'll throw a temper tantrum — timed to cause you the most embarrassment, inconvenience and humiliation — in order to get his way. She'll threaten to go home with someone else, someone who knows how to 'treat her right'. He may even go so far as to flirt — or worse — with other people in front of you just to show that he has options that you don't… and he'll pull the trigger if you aren't giving him what he wants. She knows all of your sore spots and weaknesses and she won't hesitate to exploit them if it means getting you to give in.

It's a long string of exercises in breaking down your will; before too long, you're giving them everything they want because it's so much less trouble in the long run than if you stand up for yourself.

You're Always Having To Apologize For Them

Sometimes it just seems like *nobody* understands your sweetie like you do. Sure, the way he acts may look off-putting to someone who isn't familiar with your relationship dynamic, but if they just knew what he was really like they'd realize it's actually not *that* bad. And sure, maybe she acted unconscionably rude to your family but they just have to understand that she didn't mean it like that… she was just stressed. Or tired. Or has food allergies. Or any number of a host of other issues that magically excuse everything that she does that piss your friends off.

In fact, if you had to stop and think about it, you'd realize that you're having to spend most of your time apologizing for him or trying to explain that she's not so bad once you get to know him and your friends should just give him another chance, y'know?

This is one of the classic signs that you're dating someone who's absolutely wrong for you. It's also, perversely enough, one of the hardest to recognize because you've convinced yourself that everything is understandable and there's a perfectly reasonable explanation for everything that means nothing is as bad as it seems.

It can be very difficult to take an honest, dispassionate look at the state of your relationship; you rarely have the emotional distance and perspective to be completely honest and accurate. Worse, there are cognitive biases that make it hard to want to be honest with yourself about things; you've spent so much time in the relationship that admitting that no, it's *not* healthy would be tacit to admitting that all this time had been wasted. And so you create an elaborate network of ways to excuse their behavior against you.

But your friends *don't* have those same biases. They aren't as invested in your relationship for the relationship's sake, they're invested in *you*... and what they're seeing is your partner is treating you like *shit*. This is why your friends are often your best metric when it comes to gauging the health of your relationship. Sometimes they're capable of seeing things that you're just too close to see yourself. Yes, there will be times when they just straight up dislike the person you're dating, but when you're perpetually having to try to convince them that no, your girlfriend really isn't as bad as all that, it's a sign that something's rotten in the state of Denmark.

Nobody's saying that relationships are democracies and your friends certainly don't have veto power over who you date, but when the majority of your friends can't stand your partner, the odds are good that somebody's missing something.

And that somebody's you.

Thou Shalt Have No Other Friends Before Them

Everybody in a new relationship goes through a period where they spend every waking hour with their new snuggle-bunny, annoying their nearest and dearest with their sudden chronic unavailability. You're both too caught up in that new relationship energy to bother putting pants back on, never mind notice that you've been neglecting your friends. But there comes a point where your absence goes beyond "guess they can't stop bangin'" and deep into "blink twice if you're being held hostage" territory.

While your relationship with your partner is important, it's equally important that you have a life outside of your relationship. There's a line between when your boyfriend is your best friend and when he's your only friend. Sometimes it's just a case of the two of you becoming so entwined in each other's lives that you've become emotional conjoined twins, unable to function without the other for long before melting into a puddle of codependency.

Other times, you may find that they've taken an active hand in separating you from your friends.

It's actually shockingly easy to separate people from their friends. Like the frog in a boiling pot of water, you simply don't notice it because it's a gradual process, creeping up on you until you look up and realize how long it's been since you've seen any of your buddies. He may have started a whisper-campaign, bad-mouthing your friends and planting the seeds of mistrust. "You know Angela is talking about you behind your back, right?" "It was cute before, but Zack's attempts at trying to steal you away from me are really starting to get on my nerves."

Alternately, she may make a point of just demanding so much of your time and attention that you simply don't have enough energy to burn or hours in the day to actually do anything besides dance in attendance on her. Or he may just disapprove of your friends and subtly but inexorably punish you for spending time with them; never anything you can point to without seeming petty or silly, but you know that going out for beers with the guys or hanging with them after class is going to lead to another uncomfortable night at home. Maybe they won't yell or throw things... but they'll sure as shit make sure you know that you done goofed and you're going to have to make amends.

This is an incredibly common tactic among abusers. Isolating you from your friends and family is a key part of how they maintain control over you. Separating you from your social circles — or social circles that they don't control — helps ensure that there aren't any dissenting voices to contradict the bullshit you've been fed or to protest their treatment of you. It also helps make sure that you don't have any social support or resources if you *do* start thinking of leaving them. The very real fear of being alone and disconnected is can keep people locked into relationships they might otherwise leave.

It's important to note that most of the symptoms of a toxic relationship aren't *overt*. A toxic partner will rarely rant and rave, throw things or otherwise act like the villain in a Lifetime Original Movie. Most of the time it's insidious and subtle, and they'll simply weaponize their disapproval and your sense of guilt, making you feel small, insignificant and worthless. They will convince you that it's all in your head, that you're being unreasonable or silly.

This is why it's important to trust your instincts, and the instincts of your friends. Sometimes that nagging feeling that something is wrong is *entirely* correct. Sometimes the problem isn't you; it's that the relationship is toxic and you need to get the hell out.

---

[1] For the record, if you're relating to people in songs by The Offspring, that's not a good sign.

FOURTEEN

YOU'VE BEEN CHEATED ON. NOW WHAT?

The Risk of Infidelity is Very Real

OUT OF THE many perils that couples face over the course of their relationships, the risk of someone being cheated on is one of the most common – and most anxiety-producing. Even in the happiest of relationships, the specter of infidelity can slip in unnoticed like Banquo's ghost. Infidelity within a relationship is one of the few sins that almost everybody agrees as being always wrong – upwards of 80% of people will tell you so. And yet cheating and being cheated on happens far more frequently than one might expect. Exact numbers are hard to gather – as you might imagine, cheaters are unlikely to self-report, especially if friends or family members are around – but the estimated numbers range from 30% to a mind-boggling 70%.

But while being cheated on may be seen as a universal negative, the question of what to do when your partner's been unfaithful is a tough one. In many cases, trying to piece things together after an infidelity can be worse and more damaging to the relationship than the act itself.

It's very easy to decide what to do in the abstract — drop them like a bad habit, destroy their shit, stand by your man, forgive and forget, etc — and to armchair quarterback other people's marriages[1]. But when it's *your* relationship, what seemed so clear-cut and simple before suddenly becomes much more complicated.

So what's the right choice when it comes to dealing with being cheated on? What is the best way to heal afterwards? If your partner cheats on you, is it better to adopt a zero-tolerance policy or to put it all behind you?

Regardless of which you ultimately decide, there are a number of things you want to understand when you're dealing with the aftermath of your partner's affair.

You Don't Want The Gory Details

The first and most important thing about handling the aftermath of being cheated on is self care. Discovering that your partner was cheating on you is incredibly painful. It's a blow, not just to our ego or to the sanctity of our relationship but to the very core of who we are as individuals. We frequently define ourselves by our relationships and make our partners the center of our world; they become our best friends, our primary source of emotional support and intimacy. It becomes a part of who we are — we are not just ourselves but part of a gestalt entity like the world's squishiest Voltron.

Your partner cheating on you blows this part of your identity apart. Suddenly this core component that defines you has been called into question. Now everything you thought you knew is wrong; this part of your life that brought you security and joy has been shown to be a lie, leaving you to wonder how much *else* of your life is false.

One of the most common things people who discover their partner's infidelity say is "I thought I knew you." The unspoken part of that sentence is that, in not knowing their partner, they also no longer know what to think of their relationship is and – by extension – who *they* are now. It throws everything into disarray and damages your soul and self-esteem.

When you're dealing with the aftermath of discovering that your partner cheated on you, then you want to surround yourself with people who care for you and support you – people who can help ease the pain and salve your wounds. These people — your "Team You"[2], will be a balm for your soul, and you will want to keep them close.

What you *don't* want to do is make things worse by asking for the details. That desire to know more is completely natural; it's part of the urge to understand what seems inexplicable. There's an entirely understandable impulse to believe that knowing more might make the act more comprehensible or less painful.

It won't.

Knowing who it was, when it started, what they did and where, why *that* person… there is almost no answer that your partner can give you that won't gouge out parts of your soul. Everyone who's discovered their partner's indiscretions almost always says the same thing: "I wish I'd never found out." Processing the fact that your partner has been sleeping with someone else is painful enough in and of itself. Asking for the details will only give you even more things to torture yourself with and images that will never leave your head. Ignorance isn't exactly bliss but, in this case, it's a hell of a lot less painful.

If you want to understand, then you don't want the "whats" or "hows", you want the "whys" – the motivation behind the affair.

Why? Well that's because...

Most Affairs Aren't About Sex

Despite the seeming obviousness of it, most infidelities *aren't* about sex. More often than not, when one partner strays, there are reasons beyond a wandering eye or an inability to keep it in their pants. Don't get me wrong: there are many occasions where someone has just given into temptation or who simply wanted to bang somebody else. However, in most cases, the sex and the betrayal are often *symptoms* of an underlying cause, not the cause in and of itself.

In focusing on the act, we miss the forest for the trees. Cheat-proofing your relationship isn't as simple as constantly upping the crazy sex you're into or fucking your partner into a coma; in fact, this belief tends to end up unfairly assigning at least part of the blame to the other partner who's been cheated on.

Similarly, having been cheated on isn't a sign that there's something wrong with your relationship. There are many, many people out there who consider themselves monogamous, who would swear up and down that their relationships are perfectly happy, but end up crossing a line they never imagined that they'd even *encounter* in the first place.

For some adulterers, the infidelity is triggered by a desire for novelty or to recapture the spark and excitement that defines a new relationship. Some people strike up affairs because they want to feel desirable, to know that others still want them. For other people, it's about the rush of doing something forbidden, the thrill of risk and the danger of being caught. For still others, it's about boredom and wanting to shake things up – even if it ends up hurting themselves and the people they care about.

Some have affairs because they're rebelling against a belief about themselves or the values they grew up with, while others may be reacting to the pain of previous relationships. Some are trying to recapture a lost sense of self while others are making up for opportunities they believe they'd missed.

Other times, it's a matter of one partner simply panicking and lashing out in a way that they feel hurts the most. For some people, cheating on their partners is a way of punishing them or getting revenge for some slight. Even if the other partner never learns about the affair, that secret knowledge serves as a sort of reprisal, a trump card that can be dealt out at any time.

Then there are those who use affairs as motivation to get out of relationships that were otherwise dead or dying. They may not realize the relationship was over — or that they were ready to leave — until they knew that there was someone else waiting for them. Other people who've had affairs were actually slamming their hands on the relationship self-destruct button — it was an affair as an act of self-sabotage, as a weapon of last resort, or even just because they're afraid and they would rather hit the eject button than face down their fears.

This doesn't *excuse* the affair… but it *does* make *explain* it.

It's important to remember this because…

Not All Affairs Are Created Equal

As painful as it might be, one of the things that needs to be considered in the wake of discovering that you've been cheated on is the circumstance of the affair itself.

It's very easy to assume that being cheated on is a black-or-white issue — either your partner betrayed you or they didn't. We have a mental image of what a cheater looks like and why they do what they do: they're selfish, they're predatory, they're egotistical, they don't "really" care about their partner, etc. But while the cartoon villain in our heads is easy to rail against, in practice there tend to be levels of nuance and context that change the equation. With that additional information, those easy, obvious answers shift and become incredibly complicated after all.

For example, there's a significant difference between someone who slipped up in a moment of weakness versus a serial cheater. One of the things that we don't like to talk about when it comes to relationships is that while monogamy is very difficult, culturally we're expected to perform it *perfectly*. As I have said before: being in a monogamous relationship means that you've chosen not to sleep with other people; it doesn't mean that you don't *want* to and managing that desire can be tricky at the best of times. The tale of someone slipping up after their inhibitions have been lowered and their judgement impaired by a few drinks while out with friends is one of the most common stories out there. So, too, are moments of weakness during times of conflict in the relationship and office flirtations that crossed a line.

It's very easy to stand in judgement and say that they never should have put themselves in those circumstances in the first place... until we look back at the times when *we* have put ourselves in situations that could have turned out just as badly. We all have moments where we've made poor decisions or — knowingly or unknowingly — put ourselves in temptation's path. There but by the grace of God, after all.

These moments of bad judgement tend to be affairs of

circumstance — once in a lifetime events where *everything* aligned just so and led to an infidelity and are unlikely to ever be repeated. They also tend to be moments that the participants regret having happened in the first place. More often than not, the participants in the affair would rather pretend that the event never occurred and shove the entire thing into a deep dark hole in their memories, never to be spoken of again.

Contrast this with the serial adulterer who regularly cheats on his or her partner with no real regard for their feelings; the crimes are similar but the circumstances and motivations are *entirely* different. Yes, it's easy to talk about willpower or morals or avoiding temptation in the first place, but humans are fallible. We all fall to temptation or impulse or poor judgement at one point or another; frequently, it's how we learn. We're imperfect beings of flesh and bone, not plaster saints.

Another frequent case is the individual in a sexless relationship, either due to circumstance or by one partner's unilaterally deciding to end their sex life. They may have any number of reasons why they don't just leave — ranging from financial ties to the fact that they may still love their partner — but they still have needs that aren't being met. Someone who's caring for a sick or handicapped partner, for example, may not *want* to leave; at this point, a discrete affair often can be part of how they're able to stay in the relationship and keep taking care of their loved ones.

Again: it's easy to stand in judgement and say that you would do better in those circumstances. But that's the abstract; until you're faced with those same circumstances, it's impossible to say exactly how *you* might respond. Perhaps you might do the honorable thing... but sometimes what seems honorable in the abstract isn't the same thing as the best or least painful choice.

Don't get me wrong: I don't say this to excuse people who've committed infidelities. A betrayal is still a betrayal. Nor is this to say that being cheated on hurts less if it were a one-off event brought on poor judgement. However, someone who had one too many drinks after a decade of perfect fidelity is hardly the same as the partner who sees commitment as an inconvenience to be overcome, a partner as someone who stands in the way of their desire and faithfulness as something that happens to other people.

This, then, asks the next question…

Is It Worth Ending Your Relationship Over?

Part of the self-care that you will want to practice in the wake of discovering that your partner has cheated on you is to get some time and distance. You're going to have some difficult decisions to make and you *will* need time to process, to grieve, and to heal. In the immediate moment, things are incredibly painful and raw; your emotions are likely riding pretty high and you're more apt to respond out of pain and anger and sadness. This is, needless to say, not the greatest headspace to be in when you're trying to make significant decisions. Deciding on the future of your relationship with your partner is serious business and one that deserves all due consideration. In the heat of the moment, you're far more likely to say or do things that you'll regret and be unable to take back. You may feel righteous in the moment, but with time and perspective, you may realize that by lashing out, you destroyed something that *could* have been saved.

It's entirely understandable that we almost automatically assume that the betrayal of the intimacy, the commitment and the identity of our relationship is the crime that can never be forgiven. As such, an infidelity is a relationship extinction-level event, blowing a relationship to ash as assuredly as a hydrogen bomb.

But *should* it be?

While the betrayal hurts, is that crime so great that it's worth ending a relationship over it?

This isn't an idle or rhetorical question; it's something that you *need* to ask yourself. Considering the circumstances of how and when you were cheated on, is the crime *so* great that it outweighs everything – every happy memory you have together, your emotional intimacy, your friendship, your relationship with your children (if you have them). Are those months, years, *decades* worth throwing aside after one incident?

Or, is it something that — while painful — you are willing and able to forgive? Is it possible for your partner to make amends?

It's also worth examining whether your ending things is what you want or what you're *supposed* to want. The cultural narrative is that if someone cheats on you, then that's it. You kick them to the curb without a backward glance. Once a cheater, always a cheater and so forth and so on. But you may find that this isn't something that you *actually* want. There's a surprising amount of stigma towards people who forgive their partners[3] for having cheated on them. People judge others who stay with a cheater as being weak, as being afraid, or stupid, or just plain unbelievably naive. It's hard for many people to imagine that someone can still love their partner, even after the betrayal and humiliation. To the disbelief of many, people often decide that being cheated on is simply not something bad enough to end a relationship over.

There are no right or wrong answers to this question. Everyone who has been cheated on has to judge their relationship's worth against the pain of the affair. Many relationships simply *can't* survive afterwards. Some of them, frankly, *shouldn't*.

But if you do decide to stay...

Are You Able To Actually Forgive Them

One of the hardest parts of staying together after discovering that you've been cheated on is learning to trust them again. There is an a natural and utterly understandable tendency to become hyper-vigilant, looking for any signs that your partner is about to slip up again and either catch them in the act or somehow head the affair off at the pass.

The problem is that this behavior is more likely to *end* a relationship than to save it – and in doing so, cause even more pain in the process.

A relationship without trust isn't a relationship; it's just one person trying to regulate another person's behavior. While it's perfectly justified to be less trusting in the aftermath of an affair, part of repairing the relationship is *rebuilding* that trust. This is by necessity a two-sided undertaking; your partner earns that trust back by demonstrating that they're worthy of that trust while you *allow them to do so* and learn to let yourself trust them again.

This is, of course, predicated on the idea that both parties are acting in good faith. After all, someone who's only going through the motions of being trustworthy is someone you should kick to the curb at the first available opportunity. At the same time, though, it's unfair, even needlessly cruel, to ask someone to try and try to re-earn your trust if you can't or won't ever give it back to them. If you are always going to be looking for signs that they're cheating, or about to cheat, or might be thinking of cheating, then you simply don't trust them.

At this point, it's better just to end things instead of prolonging both of your misery.

Similarly, part of forgiving your partner is to actually forgive them and let the wound heal over rather than continually picking at the scab. Constantly holding their mistakes over their heads (again, assuming a good faith effort at fixing things on their part) isn't forgiveness, it's just needless cruelty. If they're working to make amends and you pull out their past deeds like a weapon, then all that's happened is that is that you've thrown their love and effort back in their face. A healthy relationship can't survive that sort of behavior. Yes, they hurt you, perhaps badly; that doesn't justify shitty behavior in return on your part, especially if they're trying to repair the damage they caused.

Either actually forgive them or end it cleanly.

What Is It Going to Take to Fix Things

The last question that needs to be asked: if you're willing to try to give your relationship another chance, then what do you need from your partner to fix things?

Obviously, the affair needs to end. That goes without saying. But the healing can't start until the injury is observed and addressed; until then, it's just a wound that will fester over time. As such, the first thing that they need to take ownership of is that they have wronged you and to express their remorse for causing you pain.

The next thing they need to do is to show their willingness to fix things by being proactive in earning back your trust. It's almost impossible to learn to trust a cheating partner again if you are the one constantly having to monitor them. They have to be the ones maintaining the boundaries, proving their good intentions and demonstrating their trustworthiness of their own free will. When the restrictions are imposed upon them from the outside (I.e. From you), then it's all too common to for their behavior to become "what do I have to do to not get in trouble". Being proactive, on the other hand, demonstrates a genuine desire to change and fix things.

But the final step in repairing a relationship takes the two of you to work in tandem. Those potential causes and triggers I mentioned earlier become questions that need to be answered. What did this mean for you, what did they feel they lacked or needed that they weren't finding here, what do they value in your relationship... those are ones you need to ask and to resolve together, because they will define what changes between the two of you.

An affair does mean that the relationship is over, in a way, even if you *don't* end things; your relationship has irrevocably changed. It's no longer what it once was and now you have to decide what it will be going forward.

Things won't be the way they were, but that doesn't mean that the relationship is damaged, flawed or inferior, just *different*.

There will be hurt. There will be sadness. But if you decide it's worth working through it all, sometimes that difference is what makes things *stronger*.

---

[1] See: Clinton, Hillary

[2] Hat tip to Jennifer "Captain Awkward" Peepas for the term.

[3] See also: almost every political or celebrity couple who stay together after an affair.

FIFTEEN

HOW TO TELL THE RELATIONSHIP IS OVER

When Is it Time To Break Up?

I'M NOT GOING to lie to you: break ups happen. It's a fact baked into every relationship you will ever have: all relationships come to an end until one doesn't. Sometimes the breakup comes screaming out of the clear blue sky while other times it's like watching an oncoming train and knowing you'll never get out of the way in time.

Of course, not every relationship ends with a loud and dramatic climax. Occasionally you'll realize that the two of you have simply come to the end of this particular chapter in your lives; there's no harm, no foul, just two people who — while they still care for one another — recognize that their relationship has run it's course and it's time to part as friends.

And then there are the times when the end has already come and nobody has noticed. Your relationship is shuffling along like a zombie, putting on the empty performance of being a couple even as your hopes and dreams quietly bleed into despair.

Sometimes there's that vague sense that things are wrong as you both try to half-heartedly keep things going because that's what you're supposed to do, right? After all, it can be hard to make the final call on that break up, even when you *know* it needs to happen. However, there comes a point when everyone needs to realize that the patient is dead and there's no amount of CPR, couple's therapy, sexy lingerie, or weekend getaways that can bring it back.

Here's how to recognize that your relationship is already over and it's time to let it go.

You Aren't Communicating

There's a reason why communication has it's own chapter in this book: communication is utterly vital for a relationship's success. After all, you're not dating Professor X; expecting your partner to just be able to divine your wants and needs is a one-way trip to frustration and disappointment. However, there's a difference between communicating and "filling the air with noise".

We have a tendency to mistake "talking" for communicating and strive to cover those moments of silence with verbal flack as though it were a way of chasing relationship difficulties away. In practice though, it doesn't matter if you can coexist in happy companionable silence, or if you chatter away like a pair of extroverted cockatoos as long as you can express your needs clearly to one another. When everybody is talking but nobody's actually *listening*, you've got problems. And if the two of you can't find a way to bridge that gap, then the relationship is dead in the water.

It doesn't matter how long your conversations can go for if it's all surface. If you can't ask for what you really want or need or open up about how you actually feel, then your relationship is functionally over. It doesn't matter if you feel like it's something you're not "allowed" to want or if you're afraid that if you ask, the answer will be "no". It doesn't matter if making your needs clear will result in a fight; avoiding or ending a conflict doesn't actually make a relationship stronger if nothing is resolved and frankly, some fights need to happen.

Sometimes conflict is how you move things forward. If you don't have the emotional space and security to make yourself heard and be understood, then it's time to move on.

There's No Trust and No Forgiveness

One of the hardest things to accept in relationships is that nobody is perfect and people are going to fuck up. Sometimes the fuck-up is painful but something that can be worked around. Other times, that fuck-up is egregious enough to be a relationship Extinction Level Event.

Part of what makes a relationship work is putting in the effort to get past those ugly parts and repair the damage... but that requires everyone involved to actually try to *fix* things and be deserving of that trust again. This can be tricky after all, because the first part of fixing a problem means being willing to take ownership of the problem in the first place. If a partner isn't willing to acknowledge that they messed up, then they have no real motivation to change. Similarly, someone who's idea of "fixing" things is "don't get caught" next time has shown that they're not trustworthy. And where trust *can't* exist, neither can a relationship.

On the other hand, fixing things only works when it's a two way street. One person has to work to undo the damage they've caused and the other has to work to accept those amends, *let* the trust be rebuilt and find the strength to forgive their partner. If the partner at fault is working in good faith to repair the damage they have done, then it becomes incumbent on the other to let that pain *go*. However, there are times when people may *say* all the right things and go through all the motions but never actually let the wounds heal over. That trust can't be rebuilt because the wounded party won't *let* it.

Sometimes it may not be intentional; we all have histories and at times the pain of what *other* partners have done to us in the past may mean that pain in our current relationships becomes too much. Other times, toxic partners may simply use their status as the wronged party as a weapon, withholding their forgiveness as a means of keeping the other person under their thumb. Still others may simply refuse to believe that their partner has truly repented and changed; they remain forever looking for proof of wrong-doing, no matter how slight. At that point, the relationship is effectively held hostage to one partner's whims and paranoia while the other is effectively on parole for the rest of their time together; one infraction, no matter how minor, becomes the source of conflict and proof of how they're selfish and wrong and so on.

Saying you forgive someone or that you're forgiven sounds lovely but it doesn't mean anything if there's no, y'know, actual forgiveness involved. It's one thing when the wounds are still raw and it's hard to feel anything *but* pain. It's another when there've been good faith efforts to repair the damage and move on and you or your partner just can't or won't move past it.

If you're always looking for evidence of future transgressions or your past sins are continually brought up as a weapon against you, then it's clear that the damage was far too great, no matter what anyone says. It's time to admit the truth: the relationship ended long ago, and it's only now that you're realizing it.

Nothing Ever Gets Resolved

Of course, not all conflicts in relationships look like fights. Sometimes those conflicts are the *absence* of progress, where no matter what you do, nothing ever changes. You can talk until you're blue in the face. You have discussion after discussion after discussion. You can fight and yell and scream.

Hell, you can you can prove your points with charts and graphs.

But no matter whether you're calm and rational, heated and emotional or anywhere in between, it doesn't make a difference. At the end of the day, everything is going to stay exactly where it is because nobody's willing to meet anyone else half way. In fact, they're not willing to even move a quarter of an inch. They've planted themselves like a tree and said "no, now *deal with it*." Now you're functionally in a game of relationship chicken: your needs and desires are rushing headlong towards one another at ramming speed and the first person to flinch is going to lose.

This becomes a game that's impossible to win because either your desires collide and smashes the relationship to smithereens or one of you dodges out of the way and ends up setting a precedent where the one person gets to run roughshod over the other because, when push comes to shove, they weren't willing to enforce their boundaries.

The worst times, of course, are when your partner even *agrees* with you that things need to change. They make a show of listening and understanding. They say all the right words. They may even make plans with you about how things will be different and what they can do to make things better.For a brief and shining moment, you feel like maybe you've reached a breakthrough. But then reality sets back in when those promised changes never happen. Ever.

What happened to all those grand ideas, those great promises, those signs that your partner'd been listening and willing to compromise and fix things? Nothing. They said what it took to get you to leave them alone long enough to get back to whatever it was that they wanted to do. Now you're stuck at the awkward intersection of having yet another discussion about the matter, possibly even a full-blown fight with all the awkwardness and emotional distress that entails… or you just give up because what's the point?

The most insulting thing about these times how it demonstrates their utter lack of respect for you. By mouthing back whatever it was you wanted to hear with no intention of ever following through, they show that they don't actually *care* about what you think or how you feel; they will give you *just* enough to make you shut up and go away. The implied contempt is simply staggering.

Maybe they're trying to keep control in the most passive-aggressive way possible. Maybe they just don't care enough to change anything. Doesn't matter. Whether you can't or won't address the underlying problems, the best thing for both of you is to make a clean break of it.

You're Not Sexually Compatable

We tend to have a complicated and conflicted relationship with sex. Even in the 21st century, we live in a profoundly sex-negative culture – just one that likes to think that it's progressive. Our sexual education system is at best a glorified anatomy lesson; at worst, it's a collection of lies and deliberate misinformation designed to (theoretically) keep children from having sex,*ever*. We tell women to be sexy but not sexual – to be desirable but to not feel desire – while men are told that their worth depends on much sex as possible, setting men and women up for an inevitable conflict. Even the concept of making sure everybody is an eager participant is a new and radical concept.

Small wonder, then, that we tend to make such a hash out of our sex lives.

See, sex and being sexual compatibility are one of the most important parts of maintaining a relationship. In fact, it's one of the most common reasons why relationships end. But at the same time, sex remains incredibly important to relationships... right up until it suddenly isn't. When we complain about being dissatisfied with our sex-lives then you risk plunging head-first into a wall of razor-sharp judgement from just about everyone around you. If the sexual dissatisfaction doesn't conform to a very specific narrative... well, you're really being selfish at best and a pervert at worst.

Not getting enough sex? Well boo-goddamn-hoo; maybe try realizing that sex isn't the most important thing in the world. Or maybe you should do more housework. Or maybe be grateful for what you are getting. Partner wants sex way more than you do? Quit humble-bragging, do you know how many people would love to have your problem? And if you happen to leave your partner over, say, wanting non-vanilla sex... well, then you're almost instantly the bad guy. What kind of freak are you?

It's a no-win situation, and there's really no way to cheat your way out of this particular Kobayashi Maru scenario. No matter which way you fall, you end up feeling like the asshole. The plain truth is: most of these issues tend to result not because of any inherent perversity or flaw in one or both partners. It's not about who's in the right and who's in the wrong. It's simply a matter of the fact that they're sexually incompatible. They simply have needs that the other person can't (or won't) fulfill. They're a square peg trying to fit into a round hole; you might be able to wedge it in there, but it sure as hell isn't going to be a good fit.

The most common sexual incompatibility that people run into is a case of mismatched sex drives. There is always going to be an imbalance in terms of libido – the odds of having perfectly matched sex drives are slightly worse than the odds of successfully navigating an asteroid field in a busted-ass Corellian freighter – but it quickly becomes a matter of degree.

It's one thing if one partner wants it every day and twice on Sundays and the other prefers it once a week. It's another entirely when the partner with a lower libido wants it once a month if that. There simply isn't a way to find a compromise that's going to be satisfying to both partners; the mismatch in their relative horniness is simply going to be a bridge too far.

Similarly, there can be differences in the *kinds* of sex a person wants or is willing to indulge. One person may be into strictly basic-issue sex, while their partner may need to be strapped to a St. Andrew's Cross and told that they're scum. If neither of them are willing to indulge the other — or possibly give one partner or the other the license outsource their kink — then the relationship will ultimately fail, regardless of the strength of their regard for one another.

No matter what sort of compatibility issues you have, there comes a point where the frustration and resentment is going to build to the point that it becomes intolerable. And, frankly, being told to ignore it or "deal" isn't an answer.

Sex is a *part* of the relationship. It's not something that can be excised when it's inconvenient. Relationships are holistic partnerships, with every aspect tied to the others. Feeling as though your needs or desires are being neglected or ignored in one area is inevitably going to affect the other areas. And while it's easy to simply say "well, that's the price of entry" to the relationship, a lack of sexual satisfaction isn't something that can be brushed under the rug. If it's left unaddressed, it will grow and fester, turning from dissatisfaction to bitterness and resentment.

You WANT It To Be Over

Many people linger in broken or flatlining relationships because they're looking for something they can point to as a reason to leave. Ironically enough, this is the surest sign that the relationship is over; it's over because you're decided it is.

Something that a lot of people forget is you don't need proof that a relationship is over or that you need a sign that it's time to go. They know what they want – to break up with their partner – but they're looking for something that will give them permission, something they can point to and say "There! That's why I'm allowed to end this."

But at the end of the day, the only reason you need to end a relationship is that you want out. There is no breakup court that's going to veto your choice to leave and demand you come back with proof. Relationships aren't the launch codes on nuclear submarines; you don't need both parties to turn the keys to finally pull the trigger on the breakup.

You don't need to be in a relationship one second longer than you want to be. Once you've decided that you want out, you're allowed to leave. Don't sacrifice your happiness or your time in a search for an "acceptable" sign or reason for ending things. Once you realize the relationship is over, then do what needs to be done: end it, quickly and cleanly.

SIXTEEN
HOW TO BRING BACK THE SPARK

One of the hardest things that people face over the

ONE OF THE hardest things that people face over the course of a long-term relationship is that the initial spark — that "new relationship energy" — wanes.

It's an entirely natural part of settling into a relationship and one that happens to every couple over the course of a relationship; the initial honeymoon period fades and what was intense and exciting becomes calmer and more placid. That initial rush of passion that had you banging out on every flat surface in the house and made every vaguely empty space a potential fuckstop starts to decline and you're finding yourselves passing on fucking like greased weasels on meth in exchange for catching up on *Supernatural* and getting an early night's sleep. Suddenly you're faced with the dawning realization that you have become everything you swore you never would.

Before you know it, you've realized it's been *weeks* since the last time you've had sex together. You want to get back to where you were at the beginning of your relationship, but despite what the advice column cartels will tell you, no amount of offering to do the dishes or help out with the laundry is going to bring back that mad intensity that you had in those heady early days.

For many couples, the sudden realization that that you've crossed the sex/sleep threshold is a mark that your relationship is now in a permanent downward spiral. Now the only thing that's left to look forward to is mindlessly shuffling through Costco together like a pair of consumerist zombies looking for a bulk discount on everything that you're going to be using to fill the void that was the passion in your relationship.

The death of passion in a long-term relationship is one of the biggest killers of a couple's happiness because we associate it with being bored. It's the age old joke that sleeping with the same person for the rest of your life is the equivalent of eating the same frozen hamburger for every meal for all eternity while all of your single friends are zipping out to gastropubs and eating multiple delicious entrees in combinations that stand in defiance of the laws of God and Man.

It's enough to fog over all those times you ranted about how much you hated the process of dating. Time and horniness begin to selectively edit your memories and now you're remembering the days when you were single and the world was your surprisingly open-minded oyster. It doesn't matter how much you hated it at the time; there's nothing like being in a long-term relationship to convince you that all of your single friends are making multiple trips to the all-you-can-eat fuck-buffet that is dating in the 21st century and you're starting to think of grabbing a tray of your own.

Except it doesn't have to be that way.

While that initial honeymoon stage of the relationship *does* fade, it does so in order to form a bond that is deeper and more intimate as the two of you become closer and intertwine your lives together... but that doesn't mean that you can't still live it up like a couple of horny teenagers at the start of a slasher movie. Part of *why* it fades is because, frankly, we *let it*. Passion in a relationship doesn't just *happen*, it's something that has to be cultivated and nurtured — not through doing more housework but through your relationship together. A long term relationship doesn't mean that you're doomed to watch the spark fade away. You just have to know how to rekindle it.

Keep The Thrills

One of the biggest mistakes that couples make is that they put the emphasis on *romance* in their long-term maintenance — date nights at romantic restaurants for candle-lit dinners and soft music, trying to remind themselves of what it was like when things were new.

And to be fair: this is very sweet. It *can* help remind you of the ways that you two expressed your love for one another in the early days when you were just starting out. But while this may remind you of those lovey-dovey moments, sweetness isn't want you want if you're trying to keep that passion going. You want less lovey-dovey and more sweaty-petty. Part of what made sex so incredible in the early days wasn't the romance, it was the *excitement*. Your heart was pounding and your palms were sweaty and you could feel every muscle in your body twitch at the same time as you you tried to go slow even when you wanted to just launch yourself at them.

When people talk about bringing back the spark, they aren't necessarily talking about feelings of love for your partner, they want that feeling of wanting to bang like a screen door in in a hurricane and wanting to climb your partner like a sexy, sexy tree. You want the *thrill* back in your sex life.

And the way to bring the thrill back is to bring back actual *thrills*. When you want to recapture that feeling of being in lust with your partner, "exciting" is going to beat "romantic" hands down. And there's a good reason for this.

One of the quirks of the human experience is that we are actually very bad at actually understanding the source of our emotions. Most people tend to assume it's a strict linear progression of cause to effect but actually it's a little more chaotic. We feel the physical effects *first* and the primal part of our brains from back when lizards were still not sure about this "becoming mammal" business decides to backfill the explanation for them afterwards. This is known as "misattribution of arousal".

This gets fun because the physiological reactions of fear — that pounding heart rate, the shots of adrenaline, the way our muscles all tense up and our mouth goes dry — are *identical* to the feelings of arousal and excitement. So when we feel the physical sensations, our lizard brains think "What the hell's going on? Is there a tiger? There's a tiger nearby, isn't there?!" When we see someone hot, our lizard brains think "Ooooh, we're not scared! We're *horny!*" and we respond accordingly.

But it's not just a matter of scared or horny. Anything that gets your heart rate elevated and excites your central nervous system is going to excite your *limbic* system as well. Excitement from one source transfers to other causes very easily; we associate that excitement more with the person we're with than the physical cause. Romantic dinners are very sweet, but they don't get your heart rate elevated the way that, say, swing dancing does.

When you want to recapture that early excitement and channel that energy back into your sex life, then you need to do the things that get the two of you *physically* excited. This doesn't mean that you need to ditch date night, but you *should* adjust what the two of you consider to be "romantic" activities.

The other thing that keeps that excitement going? Novelty. Doing new and arousing (physically, not sexually) activities together gets you out of the rut of the "same ol', same ol'" and challenges you in ways you never anticipated. Just as with physical activities, getting excited by this new activity will transfer to how you feel about your partner. That, in turn, will help rekindle those early day thrills and get your bits tingling again.

So skip the romantic dinners when it comes to date night. Instead, go dancing or rock climbing. Participate in a Locked Room challenge. Pass on wine and candles and go ride some roller-coasters instead.

See Other People (Kind of...)

One of the common issues in long-term relationships is the way things can start to feel... well, same-y. Now, to be fair, this is part of how relationships are able to last. As I've said before: the half-life of romantic love is about 6 months to a year – following that, passion naturally starts to ebb while emotional intimacy tends to grow in it's place. The problem however, is that as the passion fades, it's easy to get, well, kinda bored. In fact, no matter how amazing the sex is or how hot your partner is, eventually it's – in the words of Billy Bob Thornton – "kind of like fucking the couch."[1]

As it turns out, there's actually a scientific reason for this.

Part of what makes long-term monogamy incredibly difficult[2] is that our bodies literally work against our best intentions; the dopamine spike from sex with the same partner decreases over time but spikes with a new one. As a result: we don't get the same rush from sex with our partners after a while. That's why the sexual encounters in the early stages of a relationship are firestorms of excitement that culminate in orgasms that blow the top of your head off: your body is reacting to the novelty of a new partner, and settles down as you become more familiar with one another. As a result… we get a little bored, even when we have an intense emotional bond with our honey.

This is known as the Coolidge Effect.

The name comes from an apocryphal story about President Coolidge and his wife visiting an experimental government farm that specialized in developing new approaches to efficiency. The president and Mrs. Coolidge were taken on separate tours, and when Mrs. Coolidge came to the chicken yard, she noticed that the rooster was vigorously mating with the hens. "How often does that happen?" she asked her guide. "Oh, dozens of times per day," he replied. "Well be sure to tell that to the President when he comes by." When President Coolidge was brought to the chicken yard and his wife's message had been relayed, he asked "Does the rooster mate with the same hen every time?" "Oh no," said the guide, "it's a different hen every time."

"Please tell that to Mrs. Coolidge," replied the President.

It's an old joke but one with a kernel of truth in it: mammals have an instinctual need for novelty when it comes to sex. Male rats, after having mated with the receptive females it's housed with will show a decreased interest in sex, even when the females are still interested. However, adding a *new* female rat instantly revived the male, who would proceed to immediately mate with the new female. Subsequent experiments found that the Coolidge effect was present in females as well; introducing a new male into the mix would cause the female to have renewed interest in sex.

This makes monogamous relationships exceptionally difficult; we are literally not built for monogamy, and often we find our relationships in conflict with what our junk want. Our hearts may want exclusivity, but our genitals want novelty.

The problem is that novelty is very hard to come by in long-term relationships; when you've been with someone for any length of time, you tend to know them very well. Even when you're trying to shake things up a little – new positions, role-playing, what-have-you – you're still dealing with the person you know inside and out[3].

Obviously, the answer is "open relationships for everyone!"

OK, I'm only *partially* joking; couples who have opened up their relationships have reported increased levels of desire for their primary partner as well as greater sexual satisfaction. However, open relationships are challenges in and of themselves and a subject that requires more in depth discussion than is really possible over the course of this book. If non-monogamy is something you and your partner may be interested in, I would suggest reading *Opening Up - A Guide to Creating and Sustaining Open Relationships* by Tristan Taormino[4] and *More Than Two: A Practical Guide To Ethical Polyamory* by Franklin Beaux and Eve Rickert[5].

However, beating the Coolidge effect doesn't mean that the only solution is to sleep with other people. If you'll recall, I mentioned that excitement is transferable. This includes *sexual* excitement that you've built up elsewhere.

Part of what kills passion in a long term relationship is *feeling* undesired. A lot of our passion for our partner comes in a self-reinforcing loop; we get turned on by *their* desire for *us* and vice versa. When that feeling of desire and being desired begins to wane, the cycle reverses; their lack of interest feeds into *our* lack of interest, which perpetuates that lack of sexy-times.

That's why one of the ways of overcoming the drop in sexual interest is to build up sexual excitement *elsewhere* and redirect into the actual relationship. That is: you get all hot and bothered and bringing it home to your partner. You are — to abuse an awkward metaphor — building an appetite elsewhere but coming home to eat.

Don't get me wrong: I'm not saying that the best way to rekindle your desire for one another is to go out and skirt the line of infidelity with a stranger before coming home to your partner — although that *can* work. I'm saying that you build up your sexual tension and arousal elsewhere.

One method is to watch porn together. The variety of actors and actresses — not to mention scenarios, kinks and so-on — offered by online porn can trigger that novelty switch in your brain, even though you're taking that arousal brought on by others and plowing it[6] into your partner. If traditional porn is a turn off for you or your partner — which is neither uncommon, nor unreasonable — then you might consider sexy alternatives like Beautiful Agony or Make Love Not Porn instead.

Other ways of building up that sexual charge might include taking a girls' or guys' night out to go party with your friends and flirt with strangers like you were single again before coming back home and discharging that erotic energy in your relationship. It might entail a trip to a strip club — together or separately. It might even be something as relatively tame as social dancing where switching partners frequently (such as in swing, salsa or country dancing) is expected.

Let that feeling of attraction and sexual novelty get the you charged up and feeling like you're a sexual tyrannosaurus again… before you head home with your honey and tear each other's clothes off.

Challenge Yourselves

Speaking of novelty and thrills…

Part of the thrill of new relationship energy is the novelty of getting to know one another; there are always new and intriguing layers to uncover when you're just starting out as a couple. Part of a long-term relationship means that over time, you've gotten to know your partner on an incredibly deep level, almost as well as you know yourself. As a result, it can feel as though there's nothing new; you know each other so well that you can practically read one another's minds and predict their reactions with 100% certainty.

So how do you overcome this level of familiarity and bring back that feeling of seeing them for the first time?

By facing down difficult tasks together. Psychologists at the University of North Carolina studying long-term relationships have found that couples who overcame difficult trials that challenged their skills felt closer and more attracted to one another than those who simply spent time together. The rush of overcoming a difficult trial helped bring couples closer together by incorporating their partner's skills and abilities into their own. Much like how arousing the central nervous system can be misattributed to sexual arousal, the glow of satisfaction from beating a difficult challenge gets partially misattributed to the presence of one's partner. By successfully challenging yourselves, you condition yourselves to associate those feelings with your *partner*, not just the thrill of accomplishment.

Working together as a team to overcome trials forces you to communicate in new ways and opens you both up to new sides of one another that you don't see often, if you've seen them at all... not to mention helping you both find new depths to yourselves. So whether you train together to beat a zombie race, enter a Skee-Ball tournament or join a bowling league, working together to overcome adversity (even if it's not real) helps add novelty and satisfaction to your relationship, bringing the two of you even closer together.

Plus: you learn valuable skills that will help the two of you survive the Zombie Apocalypse.

Another way of reintroducing novelty into your relationship is to get out of your comfort zone. Not just sexually mind you, although that's certainly a good idea, but in your day to day life. Part of what makes relationships feel stale is that we fall into ruts; comfortable ruts, but ruts none the less. When every day is fundamentally the same, it all starts to blend together into a bland, taupe mush. Forcing yourselves out of the rut by trying things you might never do otherwise forces you to adapt to new and unknown situations. You want to do things together that neither of you have ever tried before. It might even be something you've *wanted* to try but have been hesitant to. It might be something as simple as taking a road trip or going camping. Alternately, it could be as in depth and adventurous as learning to scuba-dive or going on a photo-safari across Africa.

The point isn't that you need to suddenly live a life of adventure and constant excitement, it's to do things that are out of the ordinary for you and as outside of your every day lives as you can make it. You'll often be surprised by how the two of you rise to meet these new challenges. By taking these risks together, you'll find that you're seeing new sides to your partner. And when you're seeing them in a whole new light, it will feel a lot like you're seeing them for the first time...

with all the excitement that implies.

Take Breaks

Sometimes the secret to bringing the spark back is to take a break from one another.

Now before you start wondering just what's allowed when you're on "a break"[7], this doesn't mean that you're putting your relationship on hold, nor does it necessarily mean that you're spending enforced time away from one another. While having alone time – even separate vacations – can be important for maintaining a happy relationship, what I'm talking about is *interruption*.

Ruts and patterns can be comforting, but comfort is often the *opposite* of excitement. We know exactly what's going to happen and so we coast along on auto-pilot, letting things just flow around us without ever thinking about it. When it comes to sex in a long-term relationship, it frequently becomes *so* routine that it's the genital version of our daily commute; we know it so well that we practically zone out as we're going from a to z. When you're engaging in the *same* foreplay that leads to the *same* oral and the *same* sex in the *same* positions, you know exactly what's going to happen and when. It's nice but it's the same thing over and over again.

Interrupting the process, however, breaks the pattern. Interruptions in a routine force your brain to sit up and pay attention again because it can't rely on automation and reflex to get through things. Suddenly things are very different and you need to give it your full focus as you try to figure out what needs to happen now.

If we get back to the commute metaphor[8], a closed road or the train getting interrupted forces you out of your daily pattern. Where your brain has zoned out before, now it's at full alert because you have to change things up but you're still determined to get to work on time. So now you have to find a *new* route or *new* options to get to where you were going. This simple disruption to your routine means that now you notice things in ways you wouldn't during your average day to day pattern — stores and restaurants you don't pass, neighborhoods that are unfamiliar to you. You appreciate and pay attention your surroundings in a way that you haven't in a long, long time.

Interrupting your sex life's patterns causes a reset of expectations – making things feel more intense because now you notice new and different sensations, while also setting your brain on edge as it waits for the expected conclusion. After all, there's nothing that makes us want something more than being told that we can't have it, even if we didn't want it all that much before.

And one of the best ways to interrupt this pattern? Is to quite literally take a break. Have the build-up, but not the usual pay-off. Put some deliberate interruptions your love-life by letting yourselves get rev'd up but with nowhere to go at first. By turning each other on and leaving one another high and dry, you'll break your your usual routine and leave yourself waiting for that expected orgasm. That initial twinge of confusion will turn to frustration and then to near *agony* as you wait for the finish. Your brain (and your junk) will start to shiver with antici...

...

...

...

...pation.

So practice a little deliberate blue-balling in your love life. Have an intense make-out session in the kitchen in the morning right before leaving for work, leaving both of you hot and bothered with no chance to pop before you both get home. Give your partner a foot massage while you watch TV together, then stop in the middle, only to come back to it a little later. Find the activities that you share and enjoy together and disrupt it, so that you're eager to get back to it later on. Let the tension build until it's almost unbearable and you're both absolutely gagging for the release of completion... then marvel at just how much more you enjoy the conclusion.

Make Plans to Bang Like Teenagers Again

One of the best ways to build back your desire to bang one another is pretty simple: have more sex.

"Hang on Doc," I hear you cry. "I'm reading this because our sex life is deader than the chances of a *Firefly* revival; how does having *more* sex fix this?"

Well I'm glad you asked, Mr. Convenient Rhetorical Device.

Sex has a lot more benefits than just getting your rocks off. To start with, a partner-assisted orgasm increases oxytocin and dopamine levels in the brain which help solidify emotional bonds, lessen anger and increase feelings of contentment — all of which serve to help alleviate some of the causes of dissatisfaction with your partner and your relationship in general.

For another, *not* having sex can become a habit, and a hard one to break. Because we live in a sex-negative culture, we tend to believe that the only "good" sex is sex that happens spontaneously. If you actually *plan* to have sex, then it's not as "real" and doesn't mean as much as when you and your honey are just so horny that you can't keep your hands off one another.

This attitude is bullshit and it's relationship poison. When you're in a long-term relationship, life has a way of leaving you with little time for spontaneous fucking; if you want to get the feeling of being a pair of randy teenagers with insufficient adult supervision, then you have to make a point of clearing out your schedules so you can have sex. If it's so important that its lack is hurting your relationship together, then it's important enough to carve out time for it.

However, there's more to bringing the spark back to your relationship than just putting sex on the schedule. Part of bringing the thrills back to your relationship comes from recreating *other* aspects of the early days of your relationship: having to work around your limitations.

Back in the early days, when you couldn't wait to get your hands on one another, you couldn't *just* bang out at will. You had to *find* a time and place, and that wasn't always easy. You couldn't go to *her* place because her roommates were always around. Your place was barely fit for human habitation, never mind happy-fun-naked-time, so clearly you couldn't bring him *there*. You had to find ways to work around these limitations and *still* get your rocks off. Sometimes that meant having a surreptitious quickie in the janitor's closet at work. Other times it meant having to get together in the middle of the day when you had that 45 minute window when nobody would be home.

Sometimes you'd challenge yourselves with something naughty and go have along the hiking trail, knowing that people could be coming by at any minute. Perhaps you'd get worked up out on a date and try to sneak into the bathroom together at a nightclub or you'd take time in an otherwise empty parking garage or stairwell.

It was that necessary creativity that gave those early days that extra level of spice. Sex and desire may have been abundant but *opportunity* wasn't and so you had to do some lateral thinking to make sex happen. The challenge and the anticipation layer extra excitement on top of an already exciting situation.

You want to relive those early glory days of novelty and excitement? Give yourselves artificial restrictions that you have to overcome. Set arbitrary rules: you're going to have sex, but you can't do it at night, in your place or in a bed. One of you is going to pick a time and place for sex but not tell the other, so they're going to wonder about just when they're going to get fucked. You're going to have sex but you have to do it in ways that don't involve X, Y or Z acts from your usual routine.

Putting obstacles in your way and having to find creative ways around them not only injects some novelty, but it creates new challenges and interrupts usual pattern of "sex at night, in your bed, right before you go to sleep". Change up the routines and force yourself to think about sex in new ways and watch how quickly your interest reasserts itself.

Don't Let Commitment Be The End of Sexual Adventure

One of the final nails in the coffin of your sex-life is boredom. Sex, like anything else, can become stale and unexciting, particularly if it's the same thing over and over again.

However, sometimes that boredom is *self-inflicted*. Sometimes the problem in a long-term relationship isn't that the passion died, it's that we took it out back and put two in it's head like the end of *Ol' Yeller*. And the hell of it is, we don't even realize it sometimes.

Our culture is incredibly sex-negative. There's "good" sex and "bad" sex and having the "wrong" kind of sex makes you a bad person. We're taught via pop-culture over and over again good people have good sex… but "good" sex is strictly vanilla. Lovers may get enthusiastic, but any non-standard sexual practice is immediate proof that the character is deviant, if not outright evil. More often than not, when a character is portrayed as having, say, doggy-style sex, it's almost always framed as a way to show somebody being degraded, rather than just they both like sex from behind. Anyone participating in bondage or power-exchange is shown to be untrustworthy.

But of course, if a main character shows interest in deviant sexual practice… well, odds are by the end, he — and it's usually a he but not always — will be cured of it. The player will be convinced of the wonders of monogamy by healing the hole in his heart with the power of love. The freak will be introduced to the joys of "normal" sex and forswear his evil ways forever onward.

50 Shades of Grey is a perfect example: Christian Grey is a domineering, outright abusive figure who doesn't "make love", just fucks and is a hard-core S&M top. But over the course of the series, we find that it's because he has mommy issues and by the last book, he's been so won over by Anastasia Steel's magic vagoo that he's able to give up bondage forever and enjoy vanilla sex happily ever after. Not, of course, before 3 books worth of badly written bondage scenes mind you; like the "scandal" pulps of old, the reader gets to enjoy the naughtiness before being assured that the bad people were punished and the good people eventually turned back to the light of heteronormativity and renounced all the kink they were enjoying earlier.

Similarly, when we see married couples, especially married couples with children, having unusual forms of sex, it's played as being awkward or degrading or just silly. Ha ha, the teenage protagonist just found out his parents are into S&M, isn't that *mortifying?* That middle-aged couple is into swinging, let's laugh at how silly and unsexy they look! Old people are having crazy amounts of sex, how *weird* is that?

All of these little moments collide to tell us that sex in a committed relationship — particularly sex among married couples and couples who have children — is supposed to be *boring.* Young people, single people, couples at the beginning of their relationship, *they're* allowed to have the crazy, swinging-from-the-chandeliers, tie-me-up-tie-me down sexual adventures. But when it's time to get *serious* — so the cultural narrative goes — then it's time to put the spreader bars and leather away and leave the excitement to the occasional new nightie and sex with the lights *on.*

And once you have children in the mix, well all bets are off. Sure, it can be difficult to break out the restraints and pulleys when you also have to get the kids to soccer practice in 20 minutes, but there's also that cultural value of "I can't do that with *her,* she's the *mother of my children!"*

The cruel irony of this is that a committed relationship is the *best* place to experiment and let your freak flags fly. You and your partner have built up immense levels of intimacy and trust, fine-tuned your communication skills and brought yourselves to a point where you can be absolutely and utterly vulnerable with one another. *That* gives you the base you want and need for exploring your sexual boundaries and bringing new and different things into your bedroom (or dungeon, for that matter).

It can be difficult to go against the cultural narrative about "deviant" sex. Even when nobody else is there to know what you and your honey are up to, there's still that feeling that you're only "supposed" to have sex a certain way past a point in your life. You may feel like settling down means giving up wild, crazy adventures or that these sexual practices should be held in reserve for relationship emergencies.

It could also be that you may be afraid to *ask* for the kinds of sex you want in your relationship. If you've been going along to get along and keeping your true desires at bay throughout your time together, it's no small wonder that your sex life is starting to fade. But again: the joy of a long-term relationship is that core of trust, honesty and intimacy; being willing to speak up and ask for what you need could well be the change that reignites your fire together.

But regardless of whether you started out with wild sex that dimmed over time or you want to reinvigorate your sex lives, don't make the mistake that so many couples have. Remember: you're not just partners, you're partners in *crime.* Keeping the adventure, the exploration and experimentation is a big part of what keeps your sex life vital and happy.

---

[1] The greatest response to this: "If my couch looked like Angelina Jolie, *I'd* fuck it."

[2] Again: not *wrong* or *bad.* Just *difficult.*

[3] ... phrasing.

[4] http://amzn.to/2afs7YA

[5] http://amzn.to/2ahMTHs

[6] Seriously, are we not doing "phrasing" any more?

[7] And yes, Ross was totally in the right here…

[8] Yes, I acknowledge that this is about as unsexy a metaphor as it gets.

PART FOUR:
SECRET RELATIONSHIP TIPS AND STRATEGIES

Now that the depressing part is over, it's time for the good stuff: the little things that will make you a legend amongst other couples. From learning how to win over your snuggle-bunny's family to being The Person Who Gives The Greatest Gifts, you will win *all* the Boyfriend/Girlfriend points with these strategies.

The greatest thing is: they're all absurdly simple. You'll look like a hero when all you had to do was take some notes and plan a little in advance.

And to round things up, I leave you with some wisdom from one of the greatest couples in all of pop-culture. Trust me: no matter who you are, you want a love like the one that Gomez and Morticia Addams have.

SEVENTEEN

CHARM THE PARENTS

Meet The Parents

THERE ARE CERTAIN milestones in every relationship. The first date. The first kiss. The first time you have sex. Your first holiday. Then there are ones that will define the future of your relationship: the first fight. The first trip together. The first realization that your partner is a person with hopes and dreams that may not necessarily synch up with yours.

And then there's meeting their parents. Unless you're dating an orphan[1], there's going to come a point where you're going to have to run the gauntlet of parental approval. It may be a formal meeting — you're being brought before the folks for official judgement. It may be accidental — you happen to stop by while your honey bunny's mom(s), dad(s) or both are around. You may be brought home during the holidays or invited to come on a family trip. They may be in town and it's only appropriate to invite them out to dinner.

Regardless of how it happens, meeting the parents is an

important event in every relationship. Even among the most independently minded, familial approval can be important.[2] After all, if your relationship is serious, then your ability to merge into her family's dynamic will be important to your future together. Not to mention, if you're in a relationship of any length then the holidays also means having to decide just whose family you'll be spending time with...

Of course, no matter how formal or informal it may be, there's nothing quite so stomach-clenchingly intimidating as having to meet your significant other's parents. Regardless of how strong your relationship is with your sweetheart, your relationship with her family can be a deal-breaker. Ideally, you'll want their approval. Failing that, you at least want their grudging and conditional acceptance. The romantic appeal of dating someone one's parents disapprove of tends to vanish after college.

If you're going to be spending time with your partner's family, you'd better learn how to win them over to your side... and quickly.

There's Always Room For Bribery

When you're meeting the parents for the first time, you want to make sure that you start off on the right foot. You want their first impression of you to be of you at your best — charming, delightful and an utterly wonderful human being that they couldn't possibly disapprove of. And on that front, nothing says "Oh God Please Like Me" like straight up buying their affections.

Bringing a gift for their parents is almost always a welcome gesture. If you're visiting them — or even staying at their place — then it's a token of your appreciation for their hospitality. If it's an informal or impromptu meeting, then you're showing that you're a well-bred individual who actually understands manners… not like all those other idiots their pride and joy has been dating over the years.

Make sure to do a little reconnaissance before running out to get something; the last thing you want to do is, say, bring flowers only to find out that your girlfriend's mother has crippling allergies. Fortunately for you, your partner is the greatest source of intelligence you could ever want; grill them over what their parents like and don't like and plan your purchases accordingly.

Much like gift giving in a new relationship, the price/message-sent axis can be tricky to navigate. Spend too much and either you seem like you're showing off or else you run the risk of *obviously* trying to buy them off. Either option is counterproductive to your cause. Going cheap, on the other hand, can also work against you if it seems like it would be well within your means. Aiming for something small and reasonably priced — a range between $30 - $50, say — tends to be a nice and comfortable midpoint.

If you're meeting them for lunch or dinner at a restaurant, then the best thing to do is pick up the check[3]. It's polite, it's a sign of respect and it also send the message that you're able to cover your financial obligations. If they absolutely insist, then make a counter-offer; ask that they at least let you cover the wine or drinks or, failing that, dessert.

When in doubt, go with a bottle of red wine, especially if you're going to their place for dinner. *Everybody* appreciates wine. A Cabernet Sauvignon or Merlot are your best bets; they're among the more popular varietals and work well with most of what you're likely to be eating. If you want to stand out and seem a little more cultured, consider a Malbec. If you know absolutely nothing about wines, don't hesitate to ask for help at the liquor store; they'll help set you on the right path.

Work The Room

One of the trickiest issues is when meeting the parents coincides with a party or — worse — the holidays. Now not only do you have to handle your significant other's parents, you have the *rest* of their family added to the mix… often with friends and other important people in their lives as well.

Like a barely-trained soldier being sent off to war for the first time, you've been dropped into a horde of strangers with not nearly enough preparation. There's the natural intimidation that comes from being in a social situation where you know one, maybe *two* people. Now add to that the stress of realizing that you have mere hours to win their approval and affection. Your sweetie may be there to help but if you rely on them to do all of the heavy lifting, you're only going to look weak. The best thing you can do is not hide behind your partner and strike out on your own.

It's sink-or-swim time, my friend.

You need to make a concerted effort to meet everyone… without your partner's prompting. Relying on them to make the introductions may have it's appeal — they'll be there to break the ice and explain people's connections with everyone else — but having the courage and the willingness to take the initiative will help your case. Confidence is appealing to men as much as it is with women; show that you are an aggressive go-getter rather than someone who lets life happen to them and they'll respect you far more than if you hide in the corner with all of the stoner cousins.

The last thing you want to be seen as anti-social — or worse, that you don't like them — so be prepared to be quite the social butterfly while you're there. Treat it like a networking opportunity: everyone there is someone who can offer you an opportunity in the near future and you'll want to cultivate as many contacts as possible. Remember: meet everybody's eyes when you introduce yourself, give a genuine smile and a firm handshake. You don't want to try to prove you can break their hand but you also don't want to be offering them the dead fish.

The key to being successful in these situations is to be like a swan. Above the water, you want to glide smoothly and calmly through the scene as though you it was only natural that you were there... that way, nobody will notice that underneath, you're paddling like a mad bastard. You don't need to be 100% at ease or in perfect synch with everyone, but you should try to match the mood and energy of the party. If it's a more raucous event, be a little higher energy; you don't have to be as rowdy as everyone else, but you don't want to give the impression that you're completely out of place. If it's calmer, then dial the enthusiasm down a notch; be polite and present but not presenting yourself like a puppy or a college student at a rager.

Make the rounds and spend time getting to know everybody; once you've met everyone keep an eye towards where the larger groups are gathered. You don't necessarily have to be the life of the party, but you should make a point of being visibly part of the conversations. If you're naturally introverted, then be sure to give yourself time for breaks to recoup your energy. Getting some fresh air, refreshing a drink or grabbing a smoke are all good excuses for getting away from the groups so you can take a moment to yourself.

Just as when you're dealing with mixed groups at parties or bars, telling some stories can help win their interest and approval. You don't want to brag, so aim more for humor... in fact, a hint (and *only* a hint) of self-deprecation will go a long way in your favor. Having some entertaining stories of you and your sweetie are also good way of integrating yourself into the group… just make sure they're *absolutely* g-rated and present the two of you in your best light. Telling your partner's incredibly conservative parents about the time you two took acid and went skinny-dipping isn't going to do you any favors after all…

Charm The Women, Befriend The Men

The tactics for dealing with her family isn't all that different from handling guys and girls that you're wanting to date: you want to impress the women with your charm and make the men think that you're a cool guy. The only difference is that you don't want to eventually be sleeping with anyone in their family.

Family dynamics tend to fall along the same lines, regardless of gender and culture. One parent — frequently the mother, but not always — will will be sizing you up as a potential son-in-law and how you'll fit into the family dynamic; you will want them to like you and see little of what their child finds attractive about you. Turning on a certain amount of flirty charm can actually help you here… provided you're careful to keep it entirely aboveboard and *absolutely* non-sexual. Broad smiles, compliments, a leaning in for a conspiratorial remark, casual (but respectful) touches on the arm or shoulder are good ideas… teasing and nicknames, not as much. Remember, you want to be charming and delightful, not the guy or girl who drunkenly hit on their girlfriend's mom.

On the other hand, you'll have the parent — again, most likely the father, but not always — who is going to see you as a potential intruder. And thanks to gender roles and expectations amongst families, your partners' other male relatives are more likely to feel the same way.

In this case, to this parent you're not just a stranger, you're a stranger who's been defiling his precious child. Among fathers and daughters, this protective dynamic can be especially pronounced, especially if the parents are more traditional or conservative. Now not only are you a stranger, but you're going to have to justify your existence to him. You want to show that not only are you a grown-ass adult but that you're *good* for their baby. It may be that you have to show that you have your shit together. It may be that you show that you can relate to him, that you have drive and ambition; you may not be where you want to be in life yet but you're definitely on your way.

In this case, the best way to win the father[4] over is simple: you want to befriend them and flip 'em to your side. The best way to do this is to find commonalities — things the two of you have in common. We instinctively like people who are like *us*; it triggers the primal part of our brain that worries about strangers competing for our resources. By connecting and bonding over the things that you both share, you are subtly saying "hey, we're of the same tribe." I've turned around a father who *hated* me when I could talk intelligently about his collection of medieval weaponry[5]. This was all the more impressive when you consider that our first meeting involved his threatening me with a Lochaber axe...

When in doubt, there's always sports, movies and current events. Just remember that politics, religion and money are three *very* volatile and potentially dangerous topics, especially if your views are diametrically opposed to those of your partner's parents. If these subjects come up and you're on opposing sides... smile, nod and change the subject as quickly as possible.

One of the best things you can do in any case when meeting your partners' parents and family is to questions. One universal truth is that interes*ted* is interest*ing*. We appreciate people who show an interest in us and want to know what *we* think. By showing an interest in your partners' parents' opinions and experiences, you'll win them over to your side, fast.

Be An Active Participant

One of the most important factors when it comes to meeting your partner's parents is very simple: you want them to believe that you're happy to meet them. Even if you have to fake it.

Whether it's at a nice restaurant or a family gathering, there's nothing more unpleasant than a somebody who seems like they don't want to be there. The grudging presence who barely participates in the conversation or who only talks about themselves. The antisocial guy who's holding himself off from everyone else at the party. The woman who gives off the "only here because I'm obliged to be," or "would rather be anywhere else," vibe.

So even if this meeting is something you're tolerating under the promise of absolutely *mind*-blowing sex later, you need to plaster on a smile and show as much interest in your partner, their parents and *everything* about them. Being an active participant is crucial for making a good first impression; otherwise they're going to come away wondering what the hell their kid was thinking with you and their *next* date will have the bar set so low, they'll be able to step over it.

In that first meeting, here's what you want to focus on: what his or her parents do, how'd they meet, what your partner was like growing up... you want them to believe that they're the most fascinating people in the world. When they ask about you, be willing to talk, but see if you can connect it to *them*. Ask her parents for their opinions or advice on things. Find those commonalities I told you to look for and relate to them.

If you're meeting them at their house or you're visiting during the holidays, then you want to fit into the routine of the family as seamlessly as you possibly can.   Ask how you can help whenever possible. Make sure that you offer to be involved in anything that may be going on. If there's an impromptu touch-football game, then you'd better make sure to be in the huddle. If some people decide that they want to play a few rounds of Texas Hold 'Em, then you should be willing to ante up and get dealt in. Everybody's gathering to watch the big game? Well, pull up a seat and get ready to cheer for the home team.

You don't have to be good at whatever the others are doing, but you do want to look like you're having a good time... especially if you *aren't*. Later on, when you're established as someone who's cool and a good person to know, you can finesse your way out of things, but for right now you want everyone to know that you're having fun with them and that you want to be a part of the fun.

While you're at it, don't forget to offer to help around the house. One of the surest ways to charm your sweetie's parents — especially if one of them is a bit of a neat freak — is to help with the dishes and the clean-up the big meal. If you're staying at their parent's house, being willing to help prepare dinner or for an event — even if it's just tidying up, setting the table or putting out the snacks — is a *must*. You may get chased out of the kitchen or told not to be silly, you're a guest after all, but the offer won't go unnoticed and it will win you big bonus points. Regardless of whether you take part, making the effort to fit in to to the family routine will help ensure that you're seen in the best light possible.

Keep The PDA On The Down Low

Straight talk: you want to be affectionate. But not *too* affectionate. There's a fine line to be walked here. Everybody knows that the two of you are sleeping together. The last thing you need to do is rub it in everybody's face. You two may not be able to keep your hands off each other when you're on your own but while you're with their parents, you're going to want to keep your hands to yourself. As passionate as the two of you may be, a little restraint will be seen as being respectful for the others around you. Every parent has a right to *not* know things, including what it looks like when the two of you crawl down each other's throats. Even the most cartoonishly open-minded of parents — the ones who find over-sharing about sex to be charming — will appreciate the two of you having a little restraint. It's one thing to know your kid's getting fucked well. It's another to have evidence of it in front of you.

This isn't to say that you should be completely unaffectionate; too far in the other direction will make people wonder just what's going on with the two of you. So keep the physicality at the G level. Handholding, arms around waists, hugs, quick kisses: all good.

Long lingering kisses, anything involving tongues or hands going places that would to lead to parents reconsidering that cliché about shotguns: biiiiig no-no.

Save all of that for times when you can sneak into their childhood bedroom instead.

Show Your Gratitude

Now that you've been doing so well, it's time to stick the landing — especially if your partner's parents were hosting the two of you.

The best way to do this: let them know how much you

appreciated meeting them. A firm handshake and a "it was so great finally meeting you!" is, honestly, the bare minimum. Insisting that they let you treat them next time — especially if they didn't let you pay for lunch or dinner — is also key.

And if you were visiting? Then you owe it to yourself to kick it to the next level and send a thank you letter.

The thank-you letter is a dying art. As soon as you get home, you want to write a sincere, hand written note to her parents thanking them for their hospitality and complimenting them on their home and the meal, how much you appreciate their opening their home to you and how much you look forward to seeing them again. If you have any stationary, use that. Otherwise find a nice blank card at the bookstore.

It's a small thing, but sometimes small gestures have huge payoffs. Showing your manners and a little respect and you'll soon find that their parents will be welcoming you with open arms.

---

[1] And I've known people who've actually done this.

[2] Of course, if they can't stand their family or couldn't give two shits for their opinion, odds are you're not going to be formally meeting them in the first place.

[3] Assuming, of course, you can afford to…

[4] Or whomever…

[5] *Thank you*, Dungeons and Dragons!

EIGHTEEN

THE ALL-PURPOSE GUIDE TO GIFT GIVING

The Newer The Relationship, The More Stressful The Gift Giving Becomes

THERE COMES A point in every relationship — sometimes sooner, sometimes later — where couples are forced to ask one of the most stressful questions they will ever face:

What the hell are kind of present are you supposed to get for your boyfriend or girlfriend?

It's a trickier question than you'd think. Gift giving, whether at birthdays, Christmas, Valentine's Day... really *any* gift-giving occasion can be fraught with insecurity and peril, especially when you're at the beginning of a new relationship — or worse, when you haven't had the "defining the relationship" talk yet. It's a delicate balancing act: if you spend too much too early in the relationship, you risk coming off as though you're starting to get clingy and desperate. On the other hand, spend too *little* and you look like you don't care at all.

And then there's the eternal question of "what do you get"? Do you go with the practical or the romantic? The sentimental or the sexual? How do you thread the needle when it feels like *every* gift is practically soaked in unspoken and increasingly unsubtle messages about commitment, intent and expectations? The Victorians' language of flowers has *nothing* on the complex messages inherent in deciding whether you're giving jewelry, a book or a scarf…

The longer you're together, the easier some questions get, but then you still have to walk a tightrope of sweet vs. sappy, traditional vs. original… it can be maddening.

Fortunately, I'm here to help you through all of this. So I give you Dr. NerdLove's guide to gift giving.

Navigating The Price/Relationship Axis

The trickiest part of shopping for a young (or entirely unofficial) relationship is understanding the correlation between the length and type of your relationship and the budget for the gift. After all, no matter how much we try to tell ourselves that a gift is just a gift, what you give to your sweetie carries an intrinsic — if occasionally unintended — message about how you feel about them and your relationship.

Don't believe me? Ask around; buying expensive or outrageous gifts when you're still early in the relationship is going to be a huge red flag to the a large number of people. It's an extension of the Grand Romantic Gesture, something that *looks* great in movies but actually freaks people out in real life. One of my best friends once got a ring from her boyfriend for Christmas.

They'd started dating on December 12th.

It wasn't cute or romantic, it was creepy. It screamed neediness and serious over-attachment.

There are plenty of people — myself included — who've made the mistake of overcommitting on a gift too early in the relationship. Sometimes it was an innocent mistake. Sometimes we legitimately were trying to bowl them over and effectively buy their affections. Regardless of the intent, at best it's going to send very awkward messages. At worst... well, it can be the incident that causes your honey to start rethinking how they feel about you.

If you want to avoid sending the wrong message with your gift and signaling that you might have gotten overly attached too quickly, you need to navigate the Price/Relationship axis. You have to take into account how long you've been dating and – critically – what kind of relationship you have together. The longer you've been together, the more flexibility you have... but whether you're exclusive or not will still influence what is and isn't appropriate for a gift.

Fortunately, it's fairly simple. Here's a handy rule of thumb for potential gift budgets:

1 to 4 dates: a card. Maybe a home cooked dinner and a good bottle of wine. I recommend a Nero d'Avola or old-vine Zinfandel, personally. Seriously, at this stage, you're still getting to know one another. Anything more than this and it's going to make you look like you're already thinking about what to name your kids. This is doubly true if you haven't had sex yet.

1 to 3 months: You're going to want to use how often you see each other as a gauge here. If you're seeing each other once or twice a week, then you want to consider something heartfelt and fun but relatively cheap: no more than $30 on the outside edge, plus dinner.

You're having fun, but it's not serious yet. Anything more substantial than, say, a book by her favorite author is going to be a bit much. If you're seeing each other upwards of three times a week, you're starting to move into more serious territory and you have slightly more flexibility in gifts. At the same time however, if you haven't had the "Defining The Relationship" talk – you're not exclusive or otherwise a "serious" relationship – then you want something cute and fun that reflects the fact that you've been enjoying your time together. Giving something practical like, say, cookware, implies a more committed relationship than you actually have. Concert tickets, especially for a band she likes, are a great idea here.

4 to 6 months, casual relationship: Same as above, but a gift of $50 at the most isn't outside the realm of reasonability.

4 to 6 months, serious relationship: You're in the "new relationship" stage, which means everything's likely hearts and cartoon birds and barely being able to keep your hands off one another. This is the honeymoon period – sweet and sappy gifts are going to be the most appreciated. At the same time, you don't want to go overboard in terms of buying presents – going over $75 (depending on your budget) is still going to carry some emotional heft. One of your best bets is something that you can do together. You're also starting to enter the period where jewelry isn't a bad idea – something small and simple, like a pendant or earrings – but avoid anything with gems. This is also a good time to prowl through Amazon wishlists for inspiration.

7+ months : Honestly, at this point, you're presumably in a well established relationship. You should have a pretty solid idea of what your sweetie is into and is appropriate. I will point out that at this stage, practical gifts are more acceptable, especially if you're living together. Just be sure that it's something she's expressed interest in; it wins you extra brownie points for being considerate and paying attention. One thing I will suggest is that the longer you've been together, the better it is to have at least one seriously romantic gift. In long term relationships, taking time to be romantic and remind your honey that you care is a big part of relationship maintenance.

Keep in mind: these are just a guide. Every relationship is different and proceeds at its own pace; you'll know better than me whether your snugglebunny would prefer a Le Creuset dutch oven over a bracelet or if she thinks cute knick-knacks are just one more thing that need to be dusted. And this is why you should…

Do Your Research

One of the keys to picking the perfect gift is keep your partner's personality and interests in mind. Some women for example, are far more likely to want something useful than something schmoopy, while others will love you forever if you buy her an Assassin's Creed Eagle hoodie or a Raspberry PI.

But when you want to show that you care, you want to go the extra mile. This is especially true if you're not into — or really — their interests. The more you can show that not only do you appreciate their passions – even if you don't share them – but you care enough to invest in them, the more beloved your gift will be.

Of course, this also conjures up images of well-meaning parents or grandparents bringing home a gift that's *nothing* like what you wanted and you having to awkwardly pretend that no, that gift was *perfect*. The last thing you want to see when they open the box is that plastered-on smile that doesn't reach their eyes as they choke out a "oh sweetie" and wonder how to politely ask if you kept the receipt. If you don't grok your partner's interests enough to know what they might want or need, you need to start putting in your research. That means doing more than a cursory Google search, a related-products check on Amazon or just trusting the advice of whomever's manning the cash-register at the store. If at all possible, you want to go to the *experts*... other fans. If you can get in contact with one of their friends and get their opinion, that's a great place to start. You also should check related forums and subreddits. Look around and see what people are getting excited over. Are there any products or brands that come up over and over again? Are their any debates raging about which gewgaw is superior? That will give you some ideas about what to get.

To give one example: one of my friends effectively won Christmas forever by buying his wife a single chef's knife. She was a devoted cook whose idea of beach reading was *Fundamental Techniques of Classic Cuisine*. William-Sonoma catalogs were her porn of choice. He, on the other hand, couldn't boil water without setting off the smoke alarm. But he went out of his way to buy the best chef's knife he could find — in this case a high-carbon steel gyutou. It was perfectly balanced and razor-sharp, with just the right amount of heft while still being sized for her hand... and it was possibly the greatest thing he could have gotten her. It said that while he may not have quite understood her love of cooking, he was willing to do the footwork to find something that she would really appreciate instead of trusting to luck or just buying something because the clerk behind the counter told him would be good.

Of course part of what helps when you're checking with the experts is to make sure you know what she already has... after all, buying a gamer a copy of *Mass Effect: Andromeda* when she already has it won't work, and buying the latest *Forza* when he's not into racing games is just going to mean that he's going to want to trade it in when you're not looking. The best way to avoid that issue? Well...

Build A Cheat Sheet

I'm going to let you in on a little secret. In my various relationships, I developed a reputation for somehow always knowing what my girlfriends wanted even if they'd only mentioned it in passing months ago; when they'd unwrap their gift they'd be amazed to see that I'd remembered.

Except I didn't. I cheated.

I put a cheat sheet together with their vital statistics and a host of critical information. If you have a smartphone then you have the ultimate tool at your fingertips: with the ubiquity of cloud-syncing services like Evernote, you can access any necessary information in seconds no matter where you are.

Here are the basics of what you need to have listed:

- Height

- Weight

- Shirt size

- Pants size[1]

- Bra/Underwear size

- Ring size

- Favorite color

This helps ensure that if you decide to buy, say, a dress you think she would love, then you're going to know that it's likely to fit. If you want to go the extra mile, then include the following information:

- Favorite fabric

- Preferred cut of pants/shirt

- Favorite designer

- Favorite store

- Favorite make-up

- Favorite scent

- Favorite TV show

- Favorite movie

- Favorite author

- Favorite band

- Favorite game

Want to take it to the next level and ensure you *always* have the prefect gift? Start pulling *specific* things your partner may want. Most of the time, our partners will leave any number of clues about what they want — intentionally or otherwise. You just need to know where to find them. Amazon wish lists are the first and most obvious place to look; you can search by your partner's email address and see what they may have put aside for "someday". Pinterest and Facebook also can be valuable places to find the gifts they really want.

But the easiest and most devilish trick of all is to pay attention and take careful notes. Whenever someone I dated mentioned something they were interested in, I'd find a reason to excuse myself – to take a call, make a run to the bathroom, get kleenex or a coffee or something – and write it down. With smartphones and cloud-synched note apps, it's easier than ever to keep an easily accessible running list of potential gift ideas, complete with links for reference and Google alerts to let you know of sales or price drops. Pair that with your cheat sheet of their vital statistics and you have the key to making sure you can give your sweetie the perfect gift every time.

Go Outside the Usual Stores

One of the benefits of gift-giving in this day and age? We have more options than ever before. The world is quite literally at our fingertips and we have access to markets and products than ever before. This gives you the opportunity to get unique and beloved gifts that you might never find if you're doing all of your Christmas shopping at the mall.

At the same time however, you should seriously resist the temptation to do all of your shopping in one fell swoop on Amazon and set your sights (and sites) slightly farther afield. You can find some impressive gift ideas, but doing a little more research can help you find some hidden or unexpected gems. This is one of those times when knowing your partner's tastes can let you find an incredible gift that nobody else would've thought of. If you're looking for something vintage from their childhood, eBay should be your first stop. If you want to find that perfectly nerdy gift, a site like BigBadToyStore can help you find an import from Japan that nobody else has. Sites like Musterbrand or Volante Design can provide cool and stealthily geeky clothes for gamers. If they're a movie aficionado for example, scoring a Nakatomi Plaza or Mondo poster[2] of their favorite flick or the soundtrack on vinyl will be a gift they'd never forget.

If you want to go the more creative route but don't think your own skills are up to snuff, you can outsource the actual creativity to the web as well. Esty's a great starting place to find crafters, jewelers and other creative types who often take on commissions while DeviantArt can be a place to find an artist to create a custom illustration of her personal Kingdom Hearts/Doctor Who crossover fantasies. If you want to take the DIY route yourself but aren't sure where to start,

Instructables can help you find the project that's about your speed.

Plus, you can find any number of incredibly talent artisans selling original creations that would make amazing gifts for the right person.

Experiences Are The Best Gift

One of the eternal struggles when it comes to giving gifts is what to get for the person who's notoriously hard to shop for. The answer is that you don't want to give something material. Possessions are all well and good but if you have the chance, then you should consider buying your partner an experience instead.

As much as we may like whatever presents we get, the fact of the matter is that they're impermanent and the happiness they provide fades over time. Experiences, on the other hand, tend to make us happier over time — there's the build up and anticipation beforehand, the actual payoff and even afterwards when we look back on them. Buying someone a CD of their favorite band is a nice gift. Getting them tickets to see their favorite band in concert, on the other hand, is *amazing*.

What's great about experiences rather than physical goods is that they ultimately last longer. A concert or a trip is more than just the event itself, it's also the stories that come from them and the way that even little things can bring back those memories at the most unexpected times and what they may inspire next. A material object on the other hand, loses it's emotional value over time; hedonic adaptation means that even things that are important to us become part of the background noise of our lives.

Just as with other gifts, picking an experience that matches your partner is important. Concerts are obvious choices, but another great gift might be seeing her favorite author speak. A cuisine specific cooking class, a wine-tasting class or other event makes a great gift for a foodie. A mini adventure like going on a caving tour can be an incredible experience that they might never do otherwise. If they're a gamer, then it could be fun to do an Escape Room together and see how those skills translate into real life. Indoor skydiving could be a way of enjoying the experience of free-fall without having to jump out of a perfectly good airplane. Even something as simple as getting tickets to a meet-and-greet so they can meet their favorite celebrities can be an incredible experience for them.

When In Doubt, Go For (Offbeat) Instant Romance

Sometimes you are just going to draw a blank. Even when you've been with your partner for months or even years, it can be a little daunting to find something that will not only make them smile but will say that you put some thought into this. That's why sometimes the best gifts are often the ones that are simple and romantic, especially if they're mementos and reminders of your relationship together.

Photos can be sweetly romantic gifts... but you want to go the extra mile? Do something different with them. Printing a favorite photo on wood, for example, gives it an extra level of texture and artistry that it didn't have before, turning a couple's selfie into something special. There are several services online that print photos in many different media, including canvas, aluminum, wood or even on chocolate.

Can you recreate some moment from your time together? Do they have special memories of a particular place from their childhood that you can bring back? Finding a souvenir that invokes those memories — or even planning a trip to relive them — can turn a birthday or anniversary into a magical experience.

On occasion, it's also good to just go completely sappy. One of my friends gave his girlfriend a key-shaped USB drive; he called it "The Key to the Tardis" because it was bigger on the inside than on the outside. When plugged in, it became a virtual scrapbook of their relationship together. He'd filled it with digital memorabilia: photos of them together, videos they'd taken on trips together, letters they'd written to each other, even several themed playlists that she could load up in iTunes. It was very simple and incredibly heartfelt. She thought it was the most romantic thing anyone had ever done for her.

True, trying to figure out what to get your sweetie for Christmas, their birthday or any other holiday can be stressful. But with a little thought and some care, even the simplest gifts can be the ones they'll treasure for a lifetime.

---

[1] If you're buying for a woman, then you may need to substitute waist and hip size; sizes in women's clothing are notoriously random.

[2] To be fair: snagging a Mondo poster requires equal parts insane luck and ninja-like reflexes if you're not going to just pay the eBay premium.

NINETEEN

PLAN THE PERFECT VALENTINE'S DAY

Valentine's Day: The Bane of Relationships

IN EVERY RELATIONSHIP, couples must face certain trials. Some trials are simple, easily overcome by any two partners who are strong in their connection together. Some — like deciding where to eat — task us with maddening persistence. Then there are the trials that, though they come but rarely, are so insidious that they can only be brought to us by Hallmark or Hell itself*.

I speak of course of Valentine's Day. I don't like Valentine's Day. Frankly I never have.

Whether it was the weird socio-political status games played by children in grade-school to the modern day celebration of romantic love through commercial excess, whether I was single or in a relationship, Valentine's Day has been one of my least favorite holidays. In fact, more often than not, Valentine's Day represented a day of resentment and misery.

My irritation with Valentine's Day comes from a long-built up resentment of the cultural cachet given to what is, ultimately, a made up commercial holiday. The earliest connection of love to the feast day of St. Valentine was poem by Chaucer composed to mark the wedding anniversary of Richard II – on a feast day that was celebrated in May, not February.

Then the French got ahold of the idea and turned it into a giant poetry contest about courtly love (aka "isn't it great to be mopey about the fact that the girl I love has a husband?") and it all spiraled out of control from there, really.

It is a day where we are expected to prove our affection for somebody through material goods and — by extension — to remind single people that they are ultimately worth less because they don't have a special monogamous, heteronormative relationship and they should drown their sorrows in whiskey like the dogs they are.

Still, much like being an atheist at Christmas, it's become such an intrinsic part of the culture — utterly divorced from the saint that it's supposedly dedicated to — that it's virtually inescapable; even the most well-meaning of couples will feel the obligation to acknowledge Valentine's Day in some form or another. So if you feel the need to celebrate your relationship on an utterly arbitrary day, then I want to teach you how to have the perfect, most romantic Valentine's Day.

By ignoring it.

Holy Day of Lover's Obligation

Here is my problem with Valentine's Day: it's not about love, it's about trying to conflating emotion with materialism and "proving" one's devotion via crass commercialism.

The idea that Valentine's Day is the celebration of a Catholic saint's martyrdom for secretly marrying Christians in the Roman empire is a myth created out of whole cloth – an invention of a 5th century work called *Passio Marii et Marthae* that sexed up the martyrdom of one of several Saint Valentine's by attributing the tortures that other saints and martyrs suffered. There are no official records of St. Valentine of Rome, nor was his feast day in February. The celebration of Valentine's Day is another example of the Catholic Church trying to spur conversions by coopting local pagan feast days – in this case, a fertility rite that involved werewolves, fucking, flogging virgins and coating everything with goat's blood. The feast culminates on February 14th with the sacrifice of two goats and a dog by "wolves" (i.e. priests dressed in animal skins) who would then anoint themselves with the sacrificial blood and run around the city, beating women with leather thongs in the hopes that it will ease the pain of childbirth.

Naturally, this shortly turned into "wolves" (young men) running naked around the city covered in goat's blood and slapping at women with shaggy bits of leather and followed by loads of orgiastic sex.

February 14th: Happy Horny Werewolf Day, everyone.

Valentine's Day as we currently know it is the creation of the 19th century, the commodification of the interest and fashionability of romantic love spurred on by printers and lace makers and it has spiraled further and further out of control since as people started to equate purchasing power and grand gestures with expressions of love. It has become an intrinsic part of the culture that we are supposed to buy things for our valentines… and if you don't, then clearly he (and it's mostly aimed at men – a remnant of when 20-40 year old men were considered the dominant economic demographic and the ones with the most disposable income) doesn't love you enough.

It has, in effect, become a culturally accepted way to keep score in Who's Winning The Relationship sweepstakes merged with the idea that we can buy our way into somebody's pants with cheap chocolate and half-dead shrubbery.

The more commercial the holiday has become, the more the stakes have been raised. It's not enough to buy a printed card, you have to buy a flower. You can't just buy a flower, you have to buy a dozen roses – bonus points if you buy an especially uncommon breed. In the late 80s, the diamond industry – which already artificially inflates the value of gemstones – started a campaign to instill the belief that jewelry is the proper gift for Valentine's day.

And of course, everything is priced with a significant mark-up to go with the constant exhortations that the more you spend, the more you love your partner.

Traditions that started with the French have eventually morphed into trying to exchange chocolate and flowers for sex – and then added levels of social obligation on top of it. The Japanese – who have no Christian tradition to blame it on – have distilled Valentine's day into it's purest essence: women buying (or occasionally making) chocolate for guys in exchange for even more expensive reciprocal gifts a month later (known as White Day). It even comes complete with a social ranking system — there's the expensive chocolates for the people you actually love and the cheap stuff — called giri-choko ("obligatory chocolate") to be given to classmates and co-workers. Because nothing makes a person feel better than a system that codifies "I'm only doing this because the social contract insists that I do so" into an actual material display of your contempt.

But to quote the wise sage, it's a curious game and the only way to win is not to play...

So the best way to celebrate Valentine's Day is to skip it entirely.

Celebrate Your Love… By Staying Home

Now, ignoring Valentine's Day doesn't mean not doing anything; after all, it's a day that's kind of hard to avoid culturally even if you despise it and all that it's come to represent.

What I mean by skipping Valentine's Day is that you don't take part in the day *itself*. Don't buy presents, skip the restaurants or the cutesy "dream date" prix fixe events. Take the day off… from everything. The day is supposed to be about celebrating your love for you and your partner, not about desperately trying to get reservations for overly-expensive dinners or gifts that retailers will cheerfully overcharge you for. So take the day to just celebrate each other.

Preferably naked things that involve baby-oil.

Part of the joy of love is the way that the world reduces to just the two of you… so rejoice in that. Lock yourselves away from everybody and have a mini-vacation away from the world.

When you're making your point of ignoring Valentine's Day, you want to lay in supplies early. The last thing you want to deal with is the insane mark-up that's going to hit everything with even a *hint* of romance to it — and it's only going to get more expensive the closer you get to V-Day. So make your plans accordingly and buy as far in advance as you can.

Ideally you don't want to leave the house or even opening the door for anything short of the neighbors telling you to keep the noise down. And, frankly, possibly not even then. So make sure that you have enough of everything on hand to handle ever possible contingency.

252 IT'S DANGEROUS TO GO ALONE

This means you want to make sure you have: lube, condoms, clean underwear, food, bottles of wine, chocolates, DVDs (or a Netflix subscription), snacks, candles, matches, oil, clean towels, chargers, batteries... In short, everything you need to set yourselves up in your own little world for the rest of the night.

And possibly the next day as well if you can get the time off.

Important: FUCK FIRST

I'm going to steal a line from the official NerdLove Celebrity Patronus, Dan Savage: Before you make any other plans, whether you're staying home or going out, fuck first. One of the most common — and most easily avoided — complaints that couples have about Valentine's Day is that they never got around to making love before the night was over. Instead they'd had too much wine, too much rich food and too much other, non-sex-related activity to stay awake after dinner was finished and they quietly slipped into a food coma. While the spirit may have been willing, the flesh was determined to get it's eight hours in because it was fucking wrecked. As a result, there's a tendency to believe that the evening was ruined, because not having sex on the Holy Boning Day is apparently a sign that you don't love each other enough.

So, it's important that sex comes before any of your other planned activities for the evening. As soon as the two of you get home, head straight to the bedroom... or the couch... or the nearest flat surface that can actually support your combined body weight and just go at it like a couple of greased weasels. Bang first and ask questions later.

Having sex shouldn't be restricted to the end of an evening, nor should penetrative orgasms mark the conclusion of the festivities. Just because one or the both of you got off once shouldn't mean that it's time to close your eyes and pass out — in fact, by breaking the association between male and the end of an evening, you can help rekindle the spark of a long-term relationship. Having a good roll in the hay and knowing you have more ahead of you can actually be surprisingly arousing – you may very well find yourselves looking forward to another go-round... perhaps more intense and passionate, perhaps slower and more intimate.

Just remember: if you smoke after sex, it's a sign you need to use more lube.

An alternate take would be to make the entire evening one long, grand teasing foreplay. Break out every single dirty trick you know that drives your partner absolutely wild and get them just to the edge of being unable to control themselves... then back off. Continue to flirt, tease and taunt one another all night long until the two of you can't take it any longer and just explode into an insane bout of passion.

Just. Y'know. Make sure you turn the stove off first. Because some things are a little awkward to explain to the fire marshall afterwards.

Play With Your Food (Just Not In It)

Part of the point of the evening is that it's a celebration of the two of you, so this both of you should be putting everything together, especially if you tend to divvy up the chores. This is especially true regarding making dinner: you should be working at cooking *together*. Making a meal to feed a loved one is remarkably intimate and a way of bonding together... provided, of course, that you're keeping a playful, flirty atmosphere instead of screaming at each other like a meth'd out Gordon Ramsay.

If you want to keep up the playful romance of the evening, then plan a meal that's simple, forgoes utensils and encourages eating (and feeding each other) with your fingers. Pizza is an obvious choice, but don't forget the possibilities of sushi, satays, samosas or kebabs or even just fruit and cheese trays. Forgo the kitchen table and sprawl out on the floor. Bonus points if you have a fire place.

Yes, at first there's going to be a fair amount of feeling ridiculous and jokes about SNL sketches. But once you power through that — or just laugh at yourselves and proceed anyway — it can be surprising how the dynamic changes. Instead of sitting across from one another, you're laying down together, with the casual touches and easy contact that comes with it. There's that feeling of being silly and naughty that turns it from a meal to a playful experience. You're getting messy. You're indulging *all* of your senses and having a romantic picnic... clothing optional.

Despite my disdain for the pressure to buy marked up candy, I do recommend getting chocolates for dessert, especially dark chocolate. Chocolate contains phenylethylamine which stimulates oxytocin production in the brain... the same hormone that's released during sexual activity. The oxytocin bonds with receptors in the brain, just as it does when we're in love with someone; it mimics the brain chemistry of romantic love an spurs on emotional bonding and intimacy.

Plus, it tastes great with a Cabernet or a Shiraz.

Responsibility Is For Tomorrow

After the food is taken care of... put the dishes in the sink and forget about them. Your night is for decadence and indulgence. Responsibilities are for the next day. Any nods towards cleaning should be limited to yelling "YES LANA, THAT'S HOW YOU GET

ANTS,"

Instead: retire to the bathroom and have a long, insanely hot soak or shower together. Just let the heat and the water drain the tension and stress from the two of you and just savor the feeling of skin on skin. Trade massages or just let the bathroom steam up as you relax together and just enjoy the moment. The world can take care of itself without the two of you for a little while longer.

Afterwards… well, it's up to you. Fuck again like a pile of horny bunnies. Sack out on the couch with a couple joints (marijuana also stimulates oxytocin production… just sayin') and some *Supernatural* reruns. Bask in the afterglow. Pass out tangled in the sheets.

And then the next day, you get your Valentine's bonus.

You get to celebrate National Half-Priced Chocolate Day.

---

[1] Same thing.

TWENTY
LOVE LIKE GOMEZ AND MORTICIA

How Gomez and Morticia Make it Last

I'M NOT A fan of love stories.

I realize this sounds odd coming from someone who teaches people how make others fall in love with them, but stay with me for a moment here.

Like I said earlier, pop culture has yet to provide us with examples of love stories; most love stories are about either romance or how the couple got together. To quote Patton Oswalt, most rom-coms could reasonably be called "Tryin' To Fuck." Instead of a long and lasting love, we catch lovers at the beginning of their story and are left to assume that everything just magically worked out for them after the credits rolled[1].

That is, of course, assuming that the couple manages to survive to the end of the movie in the first place.

The most famous, beloved love stories of all time all end in the death of one or both of the lovers. Tristian and Isolde, Romeo and Juliet, Oliver Barrett and Jenny Cavalleri, Jack Dawson and Rose DeWitt Bukater, Peter Parker and Gwen Stacy, even modern books like John Green's The Fault In Our Stars focuses on the tragedy of loss like a literary cheat code to make the love more poignant. It's a neat trick; we get all the build-up of the early days of the romance without ever having to worry that the couple will face the everyday trials that so often force lovers apart. Once they're separated by death, their love becomes sanctified and pure, the dead lover canonized by virtue of not having a chance to reveal that they're flawed and human while the surviving party goes on to be romanticized by their loss.

It's all very sweet... but when we're we're fetishizing the early days of love, when it's all fresh and new and exciting. We rarely see a celebration of an old love – one that has withstood the test of time and has only been made stronger. We have damned few couples to point to as proof that while love may not conquer all, it can sure as hell inspire us to make sure it lasts.

All of this is a long-winded way to say that I want to close this book out with some appreciation for the story of Gomez and Morticia Addams. When they were introduced to television the 60s they stood out in stark contrast from other couples — or even couples in modern day sitcoms, for that matter — as a pair who truly loved one another and have for a long time. In fact, whether in the 60s era sitcom or the movies from the 90s, Gomez and Morticia are, in many ways, the perfect couple... and many couples could learn how to make love last by following their example.

They Make an Effort

One of the things that makes a new relationship so exciting is that "new relationship energy". Everything is new and amazing and everything about our partner is fascinating. But what's even more intoxicating is that with a new partner, we start to see ourselves through their eyes; in many ways, we see ourselves the way we wish we could be seen. It's an electrifying experience and it inspires us to try even harder. Put more effort in our appearance. We plan more elaborate and exciting dates. We give them little gifts just because we want to see them smile.

But in any relationship, habituation sets in. That initial rush of dopamine fades away and the intensity of the initial relationship dwindles as you and your lover become more accustomed to one another. The new and exotic has become familiar, the novel is no longer exciting. You start to relax, and in doing so, well, your standards start to slide a little. You aren't as worried about looking your best. You aren't as worried that about what they'll think of you when they hear you fart or see you first thing in the morning before you've had your coffee. You don't work as hard at dating and those nights out have become evenings in. Once you got dressed to the nines to take on the city nightlife; now you're both in your "couldn't give a shit" sweats with an *Agents of S.H.I.E.L.D* marathon waiting for you on the DVR.

This never happened with Gomez and Morticia.

Through decades of marriage and even two kids, they haven't settled. They make a concerted effort to look good for each other, even when they're planning a quiet night at home, watching the best comedies Chiller has to offer. Morticia wears her best shrouds, while Gomez is never less than dapper with his suits, styled hair and carefully cultivated and groomed mustache.

They continually reaffirm their attraction to one another. Throughout the show, Gomez and Morticia are remarkably physically affectionate. There isn't a moment where the two of them aren't casually touching one another, complimenting one another or otherwise making a point to say how much they care for the other. There's never a question that they see one another as the greatest thing that's ever happened to them in their lives. Even when Gomez' ardor at hearing Tish "accidentally" speak French is inconvenient, his affection for her isn't rejected, just postponed.

And honestly: is there any line more romantic than "You are dearer to me than all the bats in all the caves in the world"?

They still treat their relationship as though they were on their first date – putting their best face forward for one another and bringing the best out in each other. This serves to actually make them happier with one another than if they'd let things slide; the opportunity to show off has actually been proven to make us feel better about ourselves. By simply making an effort, Gomez and Morticia help create a positive feedback loop that keeps the magic in the relationship.

Speaking of effort though…

It's Not Work, It's an Investment

One of the cliches about relationships is that they take "work". If your relationship is failing, then clearly you're not working hard enough. And once you absorb this metaphor it becomes clear that you're just never of the clock. Any relationship past a certain point becomes a job and you're pulling a double shift at the factory every day; – soul-sucking drudgery that eats away our time a little each day until we're one step closer to the grave. Small wonder then, that we see the effort necessary to maintain long-term relationships as tedium, forcing ourselves into the coal mines and the foundries trying to keep the relationship going despite never having time off to stop and enjoy the fruits of your labors.

That way lies bitterness and resentment, no?

But look at Gomez and Morticia and you see another way of seeing things. After all, it's clear that neither of them see maintaining their relationship as work... but at the same time, it's not effortless either. That's because they don't see it as work; they see putting the effort into maintaining their relationship as an investment. It's not a job as much as it is a garden – something that yes, does needs tending, but the results make the work all worthwhile. And more importantly, the tending of that garden is often satisfying in and of itself.

When you watch Gomez and Morticia together, it's clear that they take pleasure even in the little things that help keep them together. Those little gestures of affection — tiny signs that they still care for one another — take little effort but offer incredible payoffs in terms of keeping the intimacy and devotion front and center in their relationship. When they take time to themselves, they don't miss an opportunity to remind one another of just what it was that brought them together in the first place.

> **Morticia**: "When we first met years ago, it was an evening much like this. Magic in the air. A boy."
> **Gomez**: "A girl."
> **Morticia**: "An open grave. It was my first funeral."
> **Gomez**: "You were so beautiful. Pale and mysterious. No one even looked at the corpse."

They stay in communication. They share their dreams and concerns with one another. They take care of one another, making each other's well-being a priority. When the Addams are left homeless and penniless in *The Addams Family* movie, Morticia takes on a job to support the family without another word. Gomez, on the other hand, goes out of his way to help his precious Tish any way he can when she's starting to feel overwhelmed by the stress of their new child in *Addams Family Values*. And this is important because…

They're A Team

One of the keys of any happy relationship is very simple: you're in this together. Yeah, it's important to have some time to yourself – in fact, getting some space could very well be part of what keeps the spark alive in your relationship – but at the end of the day, a relationship is about one "we", not two "me's". Yes, you're individuals, but the point of a relationship is that you're stronger and better together than you are separately. And that means taking equal responsibility in the relationship. This doesn't necessarily mean splitting the chores down the middle and making sure everything is shared 50/50, but it does mean shouldering equal levels of the work to keep the relationship together.

In the case of Gomez and Morticia, it's clear that they compliment each other. Gomez attacks everything with zeal and almost childlike wonder while Morticia is very clearly the steadying influence with a calm and collected intelligence that keeps him on track. They have their own interests — Gomez has his cigars, chess and model trains; Morticia has her gardening, music, seances and black magic.

However, as different in temperament and affinities as the two may be, they are equal partners in the relationship. They co-parent their children, attending parent-teacher meetings, plays and recitals together.

And when trouble strikes, they don't stop to apportion blame or criticize one another; they drop everything and face it *together*. They aren't keeping score about who did what, they're focused on making things better. They understand to their core that together there's nothing they can't overcome.

They Find Glory In The Struggle

Every relationship, no matter how strong or happy will hit the skids eventually. It's inevitable; there will always be conflict and hardship. It may be a fundamental difference in lifestyles or values. It may be that one or both partners fall on hard times and this directly affects the relationship itself. There may be an infidelity or an argument that rages out of control.

But while every relationship has it's trials, not every relationship can survive them. Even if you make it through the immediate ordeal, your relationship may well have seen it's final days.

You see, one of the most telling signs of whether a relationship has what it takes to go the distance is in how the couple sees adversity and how it relates to their story. Words have immense power, and the words we use to describe our relationships define how we relate to one another.

Studies have found that the way couples talk about their relationship and the challenges they've faced changes the odds of their long-term success. Do couples talk about trouble as something they overcome together or is it something they endured? Do they see it as something that nearly broke them, or do they see it as something that they overcame together? A couple who sees their relationship history as "chaotic" or "troubled" is basically doomed. But a couple that sees the struggle as being their crucible, the trial that made them stronger? The couple that sees the troubles they face as the fire that tempers the steel of their commitment together? That's going to be the couple that survives.

Gomez and Morticia live this credo. They may be knocked down. They may struggle. They may argue and fight like cat sith and hellhounds... but at the end of the night, their story is one of overcoming difficulty and being all the stronger for it. Those fights reinforce their commitment to one another. Those hard times are the fires that temper the steel of their relationship and their devotion together. Their shared love for one another, their mutual goals and values help them steer through the storm and come out triumphant on the other side.

And whatever doesn't kill them had better run faster than they do.

"We Gladly Feast Upon Those Who Would Subdue Us" aren't just pretty words, dear readers...

Marriage Isn't The End of Sexual Adventure

One of the oldest cliches about marriage is that it's the end of sexual excitement. Those days of swinging from the chandeliers, sneaking off to bone in semi-privacy and trying every position under the sun comes to an end as soon as the ring goes on her finger, dooming you both to boring, bog-standard missionary position sex once a month, if that. Worse, when you have kids, you can kiss any sort of sexual experimentation goodbye.

When a relationship goes on for long enough, we start to see our partners (and ourselves) differently than we did at the beginning. You're adults now. You have responsibilities. You can't be tying one another up or inviting a third party in to put the "try" in "triangle". You can't do those unbelievably kinky things you've read about with your wife... she's not just some bar skank, she's the *mother* of your *children.*

But it doesn't have to be that way.

Part of what make Gomez and Morticia such a striking couple is how passionate they are. They've kept the spark going in their relationship because they've never stopped seeing one another as sexual beings. Sex and sexual satisfaction is one of the most important factors in a relationship's long-term success... and Gomez and Morticia know it.

But just as importantly, they haven't let marriage and children keep them from exploring the boundaries of sexual pleasure. Boredom – especially sexual boredom- is the death of passion, Novelty, however, is the antithesis of boredom. That novelty is part of why so many people cheat – they want the thrill of the new again. But for Gomez and Morticia, the sex has never gone stale because they've kept the novelty factor high. Sex isn't just bodies to them, it's high art. The two of them have an incredibly rich and varied sex life even after all these years because they don't see marriage as being the death-knell for sexual adventure. No matter what else has happened in their lives, they still recognize that they're both highly sexual beings. They keep their passions high by letting their freak flags fly proudly, exploring their kinks together (and inventing more than a few of their own.)

Yes, people look at them oddly – a pair of grown adults carrying on like teenagers. But that's part of what makes them work. They've thrown off society's rules and expectations about what a long-term relationship is "supposed" to be and made their own rules.

They're weird. They're creepy. They're a little kooky. Mysterious and spooky.

And after decades together, they are still totally, madly, passionately in love with one another.

If we would all spend a little more time following the examples of Gomez and Morticia, our relationships can too.

---

[1] With the general exception of Harrison Ford, that is.

TWENTY-ONE

THE SECRET TO A LOVE THAT LASTS

One Wierd Trick To Make Your Relationship Last

IF YOU WERE to ask me about the *one* thing that will determine whether or not a couple is going to last, I'd think you were crazy. I mean: trying to boil down *all* of the complexities of a relationship into one single line of advice? Did you not see that I just wrote an entire *book* about how to have a long, happy, successful relationship? And now you want it all boiled down into something I could slap onto a bumper-sticker?[1]

But as it turns out, there's an answer. And it's deceptively simple:

It's how the two of you choose to look at your relationship.

See, our brains are kind of stupid. We mistakenly assume that everything we see, experience and feel is an accurate representation of the world around us — that everything we perceive, is 100% exactly as it appears in the real world. In reality... not so much.

As it turns out, our brains have fairly limited bandwidth. We can only handle so much information at one time, so in order to free up space, our brains skip over things and fill in the blanks based on what we know and what we expect to happen. Our reality is filtered through our expectations, to the point that simply *thinking* something else is happening can completely re-write what we're experiencing.

The greatest example of this is what's known as the McGurk Effect - when the auditory component of a sound - someone saying "bah", for example - is paired with the *visual* component of a different sound - in this case, video of someone saying "mah". Your ears hear one thing, your eyes see another and your *brain* decides that you're hearing something else entirely. If you close your eyes, you'll hear the "bah", but as soon as you open them, you'll hear the "mah" instead… even though nothing about the audio has changed.

Seriously. Take a moment to look up "The McGurk Effect" on YouTube and realize that those philosophical discussions you had after a mighty bong hit about how everybody sees red differently were entirely correct.

So where am I going with this?

Well, it's about expectations. You're expecting to hear one thing, based on your visual input, and so you do. The same thing applies to relationships: what you expect is what you will get. Not because the experience is manifestly different, but how you *perceive* and *react* to it will be.

Now, the big question is: how does this apply to you as a couple?

Celebrate The Good, Endure The Bad

Since we see what we expect to see, it's important to make sure that what you expect are the best parts of your relationship. The problem is — as I mentioned in chapter 7 — that the bad almost always outweighs the good in our minds. Because we have this inborn negativity bias, the good times tend to pass by without comment while the hard times stick like glue in our minds.

That's why it's so important to celebrate the good times in your life. I don't mean just *acknowledge* it, I mean to actually *celebrate*. It's great that your partner can assume that you're proud of them, but nothing feels better than to get that little burst of validation from someone you love and trust. It's lets them know that you see what they've done and you want them to *know*, without a doubt, how proud you are. That's why it's good to celebrate life's little victories; it reaffirms that you appreciate your partner's accomplishments, just as they appreciate yours.

Of course, these days there's a certain amount of detached cynicism when it comes to celebrating minor achievements. There's no end to all of the tiresome think-pieces about how people are getting trophies for just showing up. People grumble and moan about how it diminishes the value of "real" accomplishments when we celebrate these seemingly inconsequential moments.

But there's legitimate value in making a fuss over even relatively *small* accomplishments. Being your partner's biggest fan is, in many ways, more important than being the bedrock they can rely on. Supporting your partner during the hard times is important — it's the first aid of your relationship. You're staunching the bleeding and stabilizing the patient. However, that's *all* you're doing… relationship triage. You're keeping the damage to a minimum and merely preventing worse issues down the line.

Cheering your partner on and being cheered on in turn, on the other hand, is part of what makes things better. It motivates us to try harder, to achieve more. Knowing that somebody sees the little things we've done, who knows what they mean to us and thinks that it's great that we've achieved it? That's a warm fuzzy feeling that makes us feel closer than before.

And most importantly: celebrating those little moments is *fun.* As I mentioned in my book *New Game Plus: The Geek's Guide to Love, Sex and Dating*[2], fun is one of the most important factors in attraction. Fun doesn't become any less important when you're in a relationship. The more fun you have in your relationship as a couple, the more it strengthens your connection, your commitment and your intimacy.

So when you or your partner have some good news, overcome some obstacle or reach a goal at work, celebrate a little. It doesn't have to be a giant production; a little reward or minor indulgence is all you need. It might be a celebratory massage or an extra glass of wine with dinner. A rewarding make-out session on the couch is another great way to celebrate. Even just being excited and asking for all of the details so your partner can feel like the conquering hero as they relive the moment can commemorate the occasion.

The *way* you celebrate is ultimately less important than the fact that you *do* it. That celebration is part of what programs your brain to see and expect the good things in each other and in your relationship together.

Affection Makes The Difference

While we're on the subject of making sure our partners know how we feel, it's also important to demonstrate our love and affection for one another. It's one thing to assume that our partners know that we care for them, but it's another to *show* it.

One of the traps that we can fall into over the course of a relationship is that we stop being affectionate with our partners. Things become routine, rote, even. We do things because they're expected, part of what we do every day, rather than out of genuine feeling. A quick kiss before you go out the door, saying "I love you too" reflexively... if we aren't careful, those just become part of the background radiation of a relationship. We are going through the motions, not giving expressions of genuine emotion.

When we want to manage our expectations and perceptions of our romance — keeping those positive associations going so we are primed to see the best in our partners and our relationship — we need to make a point to express ourselves. Not just to say the words or perform the expected obeisances, but to make a point of demonstrating and expressing our fondness for the person we love.

After all, whether we've been with someone for six months or sixty years, we still like to know that they're happy and want to be with us.

Let's go back to Chapter 4 for a moment and the example of Patrick Swayze in *Ghost*. The fact that Swayze's character Sam can't say "I love you," is a minor plot point; Demi Moore's character Molly feels a little put out by the fact that Sam just says "Ditto" when she tells him that she loves him. He may not feel comfortable saying the words, but he clearly feels the emotions regardless. However, it's become such a ritual between the two of them that it's lost all meaning. It feels less like a playful moment of someone who's uncomfortable with intimacy than someone who's just... doing what's expected. That feeling of rote recitation damages the relationship. Not critically, of course; it's closer to being stabbed with a teeny-tiny knife. But those small cuts and stings add up over time, and it sets a specific tone and expectation.

Gomez and Morticia, on the other hand are always

complimenting one another, always touching one another and being sweet to each other. Not a day goes by without a "Cara mia" or a reminder of how much they mean to one another. Critically, it feels *genuine*, rather than automatic. They are deliberately reminding each other how they feel and setting their expectations accordingly.

If you want to make your relationship a generally more positive one, make sure that you keep up your affection for one another. You don't need to be continually making a production of your love — that can feel like you're making a joke or putting on a meaningless performance — but you do want to express your fondness and affection for one another. Compliments, terms of endearment and flirting are all ways of keeping that feeling of affection alive. So too are little touches; not just kisses or hugs (though those are important) but the casual physical contact that reminds them that you like being with them. Your hands on their waist, your knee next to theirs and snuggling up to them on the couch or in bed… these are all ways of reminding your partner that you care.

They may be little gestures — a hand to the small of the back as you walk through a door, an unsolicited compliment — but those little gestures build up over time too, just as surely as those tiny cuts.

Me vs. We

Another key to the way you perceive your relationship is managing the "me" vs. "we" factor.

There's a delicate balancing act when it comes to making a relationship last. You're both an individual with their own wants and needs but also part of a gestalt being — that numinous "we" that you and your partner built together.

You construct that "we" out of your time together, of the life you've shared and the work you've both put in. Focusing on the "we" means that you often have to put aside your own wants and needs and doing the things that support the relationship.

This is, admittedly a tricky line to walk at times. While it's important to have a life outside of your relationship, it's also important to remember that at the end of the day, you've chosen to be *together*. You're individuals yes, but you're also a couple and that relationship is supposed to be greater than the two of you apart.

Notice very carefully that I didn't say your *partner's* needs. While that is important, that's not what I'm talking about here. Your partner's needs aren't the same as the *relationship's* needs. The relationship requires maintenance from the two of you working on concert with one another.

You both will have to be willing to sacrifice your interests and time to do things that are specifically for the relationship itself. It may be something as simple as establishing a date night and sticking to it. It may be something as fun as finding couples activities that encourage the two bond on a deeper and more meaningful level. Or it may be something as emotionally difficult as setting up a recurring appointment with a relationship counselor to iron out issues that you're unable to resolve yourselves.

You will have things that you want. Your partner will have things that *they* want. It's important that you both indulge each other's needs and do things specifically for your partner... but that's not the "we", that's two "me's".

If you want your relationship to last, you've got to remember that your "we" isn't just you and them, it's what the two of you have built *together*.

The Glory Is In The Struggle

Of course, into every relationship, some strife must fall. How you respond to those hard times is what will make the difference in the long run. Do you believe that trouble is inevitable and hard times are there to be endured? Or do you dig in your heels, spit into your hands and get ready to do whatever it takes to get through to the other side?

That choice is significant, because it could affect the rest of your relationship together. Couples who see trouble as something to be endured are far more likely to break up than the ones who treat it as something to overcome.

There are two factors at work here. The first is simply the locus of control. Couples who are content to passively endure the hard times and wait for them to pass are functionally giving up their ability to change their relationships. In focusing on endurance and simply trying to bear up under the stresses of a relationship, they're saying that they're helpless to do anything to better their position. Relationships are hard and shit happens, so wear a hat.

Couples who gear up to work through the problems, on the other hand, are coming to it from a place of agency. In trying to overcome whatever life throws at them, they are taking an active role in their own relationship. They know that things are tough — they're facing the same problems as everyone else and feeling them just as keenly — but they're choosing to work together to get through. They believe that they are in a position to fix things, as long as they try. That belief, that fundamental optimism of "this is hard, but we can work harder," gives them the emotional resilience to keep trying. They get knocked down, but they get back up again. They tire, but they endure.

Like a bird pecking away at at mountain, they may not make

much progress at first, but they keep at it until they wear that mountain away. By fighting for their relationship, they know they can break through eventually.

And it's that struggle together that leads to the other factor that determines who stays together and who breaks up: the reinforcement of "me vs. we". Couples who simply endure are maintaining the status quo. They don't commit to the "we". They continue to do the same things over and over and watching their relationship fall apart under the stress.

Couples, on the other hand, who struggle and fight are committing to the "we". They are growing and changing *together*. In taking a position of conscious effort and improvement, they're having to work together as a team. They have to communicate and cooperate. They're finding new and different ways of solving their problems as a unit and it's bringing them closer together. The times are hard, the pain is great and the stress is almost unbearable. But in working together and rising up to the challenge, they come out the other side stronger and better than they were before. They fight on because they know that in the end, it's *worth it*.

That's the glory in the struggle to make a relationship last. There will be times when it's nothing but frustration and pain. There will be times when it seems like nothing would go right if you stuck a gun to it's head. But when those times come, if the two of you look at each other, roll up your sleeves and prepare to face those troubles head on... you'll find yourselves breaking through to the other side and ready to face the other challenges life throws at you.

And *that* leads us to the most important part about making a relationship last...

How Do You Tell Your Story?

At the end of the day, the longevity of your relationship is going to revolve around the stories you tell about your relationship. Is it the story of two people who muddle through life? Or do you tell the story of two determined bastards who've fought for every scrap they have and love each other all the more for it?

Sounds a bit woo-woo crazy-pants, doesn't it? But there's actual science to back it up. A study from the University of Washington[3] found that the longevity of a couple's relationship could be predicted with 94% accuracy based on how couples describe their relationship history.

See, the stories we tell about our relationships define who we are as a couple. Those stories correspond to how we perceive the way our relationships have progressed. Those stories influence how you see your relationship as a whole and set your expectations accordingly. The more negatively you describe your relationship, the more you're predicting the *future* of your relationship together. Those negative beliefs are going to color the way you see everything in your life with your partner. They could be sitting quietly eating Triscuits and you'd *still* be getting pissed off at them; look at them eating crackers like they're not the worst person in the world.

Alternately, the more positively you describe your relationship, the more that positivity is going to influence your perceptions. Yeah, you're struggling right now, but you know that deep down, you both love each other and at the end of the day there's nobody you'd rather have at your back.

Don't get me wrong: I'm not saying that you're supposed to pretend that you *didn't* have to struggle. You don't have to act as though you didn't have hard times or that there weren't moments that *by God* you were ready to choke a motherfucker. It doesn't matter how much you love one another. It doesn't matter how much sex you have or how many separate vacations you take. Every couple has times when they are just sick of their partner's shit.

But it's how you *choose* to view those times that makes all the difference. And it *is* a choice. As someone wise once told me: pain is inevitable. Everybody's going to get hurt at one point or another. But while *pain* is inevitable, *suffering* is optional. You will hurt. You will get angry. Hell, you will have days when you're so pissed off that you're quivering with suppressed rage. But if you can grit your teeth and hold on to that core of love at the center of your relationship - you know, the one I've been talking about over and over - then you can find the strength to get through those bad times and back into the good.

And when the good times come again: how are you going to describe what happened? What is the story that you will ultimately tell about your relationship?

Are those bad times simply a matter of how close you came to ending things, or are they a time when the lightning flashed and the pillars of Heaven shook and the two of you lashed yourselves together and rode through the storm?

Do you talk about how it was a mistake to get married? Are you talking about how much freer you were in your single days? Do you talk about the hard times as though it was the worst time of your lives and it's a miracle you got through it at all?

Or — like Gomez and Morticia — do you look at it as a struggle that brought you two closer together? Did it nearly tear you apart, or did it show you that you had more work to do and inspired you both to work harder?

Do you talk about how marriage may be a struggle, but at the end of the day, it's worth every hard-fought moment?

Do you talk about the hard times and the bitterness? Or can you find the good that came from the conflict?

The stories you tell about yourselves will be what determines your future together. So it's up to you.

Tell your story.

Just make sure it's a good one.

Good luck.

[1] Actually, that's not a bad idea. Mental note: look into printing bumper stickers.

[2] http://amzn.to/2btLknY

[3] https://www.researchgate.net/publication/232601072_How_a_Couple_Views_Their_Past_Predicts_Their_Future_Predicting_Divorce_from_an_Oral_History_Interview

About The Author

Harris O'Malley (AKA Dr. NerdLove) is an Austin-based, internationally recognized blogger and dating coach who provides geek dating advice at Paging Dr. NerdLove and his bi-weekly advice column "Ask Dr. NerdLove" on Kotaku.

He and his work has been featured on Nightline, The Guardian, New York Magazine, The Huffington Post, Wired, Sex Nerd Sandra, Daily Life, Slate, The Austin-American Statesman, Austin Monthly, Geek and Sundry, Boing Boing, Everyday Feminism, Buzzfeed, The Daily Dot, The Washington Post, Kotaku, Lifehacker, NeilStrauss.com, The Good Man Project, MTV's Guy Code, The Harvard Business Journal, and many others.

Keep up with the latest from Dr. NerdLove:

TWITTER: @DrNerdLove

FACEBOOK: DrNerdLove

EMAIL: doc@doctornerdlove.com

For more more advice on dating, sex & relationships, visit him online at www.doctornerdlove.com